Paper Pieced Modern

13 Stunning Quilts

Step-by-Step Visual Guide

Amy Garro

stashBOOKS.
an imprint of C&T Publishing

Text copyright © 2015 by Amy Garro

Photography and artwork copyright © 2015 by C&T Publishing, Inc.

Publisher: Amy Marson

Creative Director: Gailen Runge

Art Director/Book Designer: Kristy Zacharias

Editors: Lynn Koolish and Joanna Burgarino

Technical Editors: Priscilla Read and Gailen Runge

Production Coordinator: Zinnia Heinzmann

Production Editor: Alice Mace Nakanishi

Illustrator: Tim Manibusan

Photo Assistant: Mary Peyton Peppo

Quilt photography and instructional photography by Diane Pedersen, unless otherwise noted

Published by Stash Books, an imprint of C&T Publishing, Inc., P.O. Box 1456, Lafayette, CA 94549

Library of Congress Cataloging-in-Publication Data

Garro, Amy M. (Amy Marie), 1987-

Paper pieced modern : 13 stunning quilts : step-by-step visual guide / Amy Garro.

    pages cm

ISBN 978-1-60705-989-9 (softcover)

1. Patchwork quilts. 2. Quilting--Patterns. I. Title.

TT835.G3317 2015

746.46--dc23

                    2014024989

Printed in China

10 9 8 7 6 5 4 3 2 1

Dedication

To my husband, John—my rock and my everything

Acknowledgments

I would like to take this opportunity to thank everyone who made this book possible for me: Heather and David at Crimson Tate, who provided fabric, supplies, moral support, and everything in between; my friends Lisa, Darcie, and Holly, and my mother, all of whom helped me with the projects in this book; Lindsay and Michele, who encouraged me in the publishing world; and most of all, my family, who sacrificed so that this could become a reality.

I would also like to thank the following companies for providing supplies for the projects in this book:

CM Designs	June Tailor
Dritz/Omnigrid	Michael Miller Fabrics
FreeSpirit Fabrics	Quilter's Dream Batting
Hobbs Batting	Robert Kaufman

CONTENTS

INTRODUCTION

Have you been wanting to try paper piecing? As long as you can use a ruler and rotary cutter and sew on a line, you can paper piece. I made my first paper-piecing project when I was in elementary school—and I wasn't exactly a master piecer then.

All you need to do is to read the paper-piecing method instructions carefully and you'll be set to make all the projects in this book. My goal in writing this book is to make it feel as though I'm right there helping you. All the fabric is rotary cut to save you the time and hassle of cutting out funky shapes with scissors, and the quilting photographs and discussions will inspire you to stretch your imagination to make these quilts your very own.

I have organized the projects by level of difficulty, beginning with the easier projects and ending the book with more difficult projects. *Any* project is doable for the confident piecer with time, patience, and careful reading of the pattern, but if *simple* is your cup of tea, start at the beginning.

A number of different methods can be used for paper piecing, but I present the method that I prefer. It involves cutting the seam allowances before sewing, rather than after. I have found that I make far fewer mistakes with this method and am able to use less fabric while piecing.

The projects in this book are written using my paper-piecing method, but you can use any method of piecing or cutting that you like. While I do include plenty of wiggle room in each fabric piece size, I can't guarantee that other methods of piecing will work perfectly with my cutting instructions. So if you would like to use another method, I suggest first testing blocks using scraps to see if you will need more fabric. Or, try the method in Paper-Piecing Basics (page 12); you might be surprised at how easy this method is.

Happy sewing. I can't wait to see what you come up with.

—*Amy*

Ombré creates movement: In *Icy Waters* (page 54), a strong diagonal feeling pulls the eye down and across the quilt, from the upper left to the lower right.

CHOOSING FABRICS

A Note about Color Schemes

Although I have been formally trained in color theory and could tell you all about different color schemes, I'm not going to. I used to stick much more closely to well-defined color schemes, but eventually I realized that this approach was holding me back. I find that my favorite fabric choices come from simply dumping fabrics onto my sewing room floor and moving them around to create new and fun combinations. I end up putting together colors and fabrics that I had never thought of putting together before. I encourage you to branch out and do the same. If the colors and fabrics look good to you—that's what matters most. It took me awhile to learn this lesson. Even though knowing color theory helps me understand why a color scheme might look good after I've created it, I don't need this knowledge to decide. *Yes, I like how that looks*, or, *Oh, that's horrendous.* Go with your gut instinct and have plenty of fun playing around with your fabric.

Creating Ombré

The term *ombré* refers to the gradation from one hue (color) to another (such as from blue to red) or from one value to another (such as from light to dark). I really like to use ombré in my quilts and used this effect in several projects in this book. It creates movement and interest—using it with purpose can help lead the eye in a specific direction.

For all the patterns using ombré, I have helped you by indicating the number of fabrics you need to create this effect. Where possible, I have even listed the exact fabrics I used. When creating ombré with fabric, you won't be gradating seamlessly—fabric isn't paint. There will be jumps as you move from one fabric to another. The key is to try to make each jump similar so that none of the changes look abrupt or stand out in a negative way.

When working with fabric to create ombré, you can use solids, prints, or a combination of the two. When using prints, the best fabrics will be ones that read as a single color overall. They could even have small amounts of colors from the neighboring fabrics. Whether or not you choose to allow small amounts of other colors into your fabrics depends on your personal preference.

In *Diamonds and Emeralds I: Madrona Road* (page 28), the eye is pulled from the upper left to the lower right.

These are the fabrics I used for *The Bachelor* (page 66). I used color cards from two fabric manufacturers to select a variety of solid reds that blended well from one to another. I highly suggest using color cards or purchasing fabric in person to create a precise ombré effect like this.

Purchasing Fabric

Shopping online for fabric is very common now. The benefit of this is that a huge selection of fabric is readily available. This is especially helpful if you don't have any quilt shops nearby. The downside of shopping online is that you cannot physically see the fabric for color accuracy before buying it. You also can't bring in fabrics or make stacks of fabric bolts in the store to see how they interact with each other.

I do both kinds of shopping—at my local quilt store and online—as needed. I value the help that a good salesperson can offer when looking for different fabric combinations. I look online only if my local quilt shop doesn't have what I'm looking for. Online shopping is best when I attempt to make my online shopping experience more like that of walking into a quilt store—I use color cards to make accurate color selection easier, and I only shop at e-stores that have well-lit photographs of their merchandise. I add extra fabrics to my shopping cart so that I can look at them all on the same web page—like auditioning them next to each other in a physical store—and whittle down my selection from there.

Shopping

If you're in the Midwest, consider stopping by my favorite local quilt store, Crimson Tate. They are located in downtown Indianapolis and carry only modern fabrics.

Looking to shop online? Here are a few of my favorite online shops:

crimsontate.com

westwoodacresfabric.com

hawthornethreads.com

pinkcastlefabrics.com

fatquartershop.com

marmaladefabrics.com

The Internet is an excellent source not only for regular quilting cottons, but also for specialty fabrics. If you're looking for something that's unique, out of print, hard to find, or hand printed, try looking at etsy.com. The printed fabrics I used for *Diamonds and Emeralds II* (page 30) were limited stock, out-of-print Japanese fabrics, but I was able to find them at the Etsy shop Blije Olifantje. (This shop has since moved to zibbet.com.)

The Dear Stella Tiny Diamonds print in *Jumping Jacks* (page 96) was also an Internet find. I had one small piece, but it was out of print. After several hours trying different word combinations in search engines, I was able to locate enough for this quilt.

If you're looking for something specific, you can often find it online.

TOOLS AND PREPARATION

Setting Up Your Machine

You'll want to change a few settings on your machine when paper piecing.

Stitch length   Shorten the stitch length to somewhere between 1.5 and 1.7. This makes the paper foundations rip off more easily.

Sewing machine extension table or drop-in table (optional)   This provides a larger flat surface and makes piecing and quilting easier.

Setting Up Your Workspace

In a kitchen, the range, refrigerator, and sink make up what is considered a *work triangle*. When paper piecing, you will move frequently between your sewing machine, pressing station, and cutting station—these three places make up your sewing room work triangle.

Because you move between these three areas so frequently, it's important to have them close together. You might consider making an L shape with two tables and using a swivel chair so that you can stitch, iron, and cut without leaving your seat.

A table-top ironing station—such as the Omnigrid Portable Cutting and Pressing Station—is a great space saver and adds a lot of convenience for all the back and forth of paper piecing.

Paper-Piecing Tools

Rotary Cutter, Mats, and Rulers

Many quilters swear that using scissors helps prevent them from accidentally slicing their fabric up, but with the piecing method I use, those kinds of mistakes don't tend to happen—so rotary cut away.

Rotary cutter   I use an Olfa 45mm cutter.

Cutting mat(s)   You need to have an area large enough to cut your project yardage, as well as a cutting area in your work triangle for trimming seam allowances. You can use one mat for both of these, but I like to keep two specific mats:

- *18" × 24" mat*: This mat is large enough to cut my yardage at the beginning of the project. I also use it to trim up my blocks after they are pieced.

- *Omnigrid 8" × 11" Portable Cutting and Pressing Station*: I use this to combine my cutting and ironing stations. For larger blocks, use the 12" × 18" size.

Add-A-Quarter ruler   The bump on this ruler means you will never slip while rotary cutting and accidentally cut your block. You can also use a regular gridded ruler that has a ¼" marking, but the Add-A-Quarter ruler makes life so much easier.

Paper-Piecing Paper

Printing the piecing patterns on paper is the essence of paper piecing. After piecing the pattern, you will need to tear away the paper backing. Below are a few paper options, as well as their pros and cons:

Paper-piecing paper   This affordable paper (such as Carol Doak's Foundation Paper by C&T Publishing) is very thin and lightweight (rather like newsprint), so it tears easily. You won't need to use such a small stitch length and you can remove the templates quickly. Considering both ease of use and cost concerns, this is the most ideal option. This paper is available in both 8½″ × 11″ and 8½″ × 14″.

Transparent paper-piecing paper   This paper (such as June Tailor's Perfect Piecing Foundation Sheets or Simple Foundations Translucent Vellum Paper by C&T Publishing) allows you to see the pattern even with the printed side of the paper down. This can prevent poor fabric placement and lots of mistakes. It doesn't tear quite as easily as Carol Doak's Foundation Paper, but it does tear more easily than regular copier paper. The downside of this product is the price—transparent paper-piecing papers are the priciest option.

Regular copier paper   This is your cheapest option, but it can be difficult to tear. You can accidentally rip out your seams in an effort to remove the paper if you don't use a very small stitch length.

TIP

If you're using regular copier paper, pre-perforate your templates by sewing along all the seamlines with a dull, unthreaded needle *before* actually piecing your block. The pre-perforated paper will tear away just as easily as paper-piecing paper.

Additional Tools

Paper-piecing thread   Coats & Clark makes thread specifically for paper piecing. It is stronger than regular piecing thread to help seams withstand the tearing away of foundation papers.

Tapes   Use painter's tape or masking tape to join together foundation papers for larger patterns and to repair any seams you accidentally rip out (Scotch and other clear tapes can melt from your iron). Use clear tape to secure the printed side *only* of foundation papers that you piece together.

Glue   Glue can be used as an alternative to pinning for placing fabric onto patterns. Any white or clear washable glue stick (such as Elmer's brand) will work.

Tweezers   Use tweezers to remove tiny pieces of your paper patterns.

Thin cardboard   Use the back of a notebook, cut out part of a cereal box, or use a comic book cardboard insert to fold back your pattern pieces.

Thin pins   Thinner pins (such as silk pins) reduce bulk when pinning through paper and fabric. I use Dritz extra-long satin pins. Thicker, stubbier pins can make the foundation paper buckle, causing accuracy problems.

Quilting gloves   Paper patterns are slicker than fabric ones—gloves help provide traction while stitching.

Quilting 90/14 needles   Use these needles for paper piecing—they are thicker than your standard 80/12 needle, so they'll punch larger holes in the foundation papers and make it easier to rip them off. Save your old, dull needles to pre-perforate paper patterns if you're using copier paper.

Seam ripper   Use to unsew mistakes or snip threads.

Iron   Use to press seams.

Scissors   Use paper scissors for cutting patterns and snips for cutting threads.

PAPER-PIECING BASICS

Cutting

Part of the joy of paper piecing is that you can sew extreme angles, sharp points, and odd shapes more easily than you can with traditional piecing methods. The downside is that you will waste some fabric. Some methods attempt to reduce the amount of fabric wasted by having you hand cut shapes that are just ½″ larger than the finished shapes in each block. Unfortunately, this can take a lot of time—and because you have to use the rotary cutter to trim down each piece as you go, you are cutting everything twice. Instead, I've opted to write the projects in the book with simple rotary cutter instructions. All your cutting can be done with a rotary cutter, and nearly all your pieces will be simple squares or rectangles.

Block Anatomy

Paper piecing involves sewing directly on a printed line. I call these the *seamlines*. The solid outer lines marked on a paper-piecing pattern indicate the edges of the pattern. The dashed outer line indicates the ¼″ seam allowance for the pattern piece.

The numbers on the pattern indicate the order in which you will place and sew your fabric pieces. You will place Piece 1 on the paper, then sew Piece 2 onto Piece 1, then sew Piece 3 onto Piece 2, and so on, sewing on the line between each of the two areas.

Sometimes a seamline will cross more than one previous piece. In the pattern piece shown (at right), Piece 5 touches Pieces 1 through 4. You will sew along the entire line.

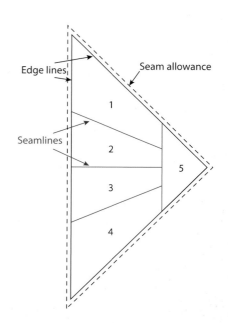

Edge lines

Seam allowance

Seamlines

Transferring Patterns

Several different ways can be used to create paper foundations:

- Scan them and print them onto foundation paper using a home computer.

- Copy them on a home copier/printer combination.

- Take the patterns to a copy shop and have them copied there.

Some printers are finicky about paper, but I've been able to use Carol Doak's Foundation Paper in every printer/copier I've used without any problems.

Trimming Down Patterns

You have a few options for trimming down your printed pattern pieces before you start sewing.

- Trim along the outer dashed line. This is the ¼″ seam allowance for the pattern piece. This helps to prevent fabric placement errors.

- Leave some excess paper around the outer dashed line. Trimming down will reduce bulk, but no need to worry about cutting exactly along the line. This can be done quickly and without worrying about cutting slowly and accurately, as you'll be trimming the entire block down at the end of sewing.

- Trim directly on the pattern edge (the edge line just inside the ¼″ dashed outer line). This way, you won't have to worry about any papers in your seam allowances when you join blocks. Just don't forget to add that extra ¼″ when trimming down your pieces after they are completed.

Joining Patterns

For some of the projects in this book, you will have to join together multiple pieces of paper for one pattern piece. Usually you will do this before you start sewing, but a few exceptions are noted in the specific projects. Before joining the pattern pieces, trim down the paper to about ½″ of overlap. Then, use clear tape to join together the pieces on the printed side of the pattern. On the wrong side of the pattern, use masking tape or painter's tape, because your iron can melt clear tapes. Trim down the pattern as desired (see Trimming Down Patterns, at left).

The Sewing Process

The easy thing about paper piecing is that you just have to sew on the lines. After you've gotten used to the setup (see Setting Up Your Workspace, page 8) and get into the rhythm of things, you'll get the hang of it. It's just a little different to get used to at first.

As a general rule, you'll always place your fabric on the *back* side of the pattern and sew on the *top (printed) side* of the pattern where you can see the lines.

1. Place the first fabric piece

Placing the first fabric piece is a bit different from placing all the other pieces. Use this checklist to make sure you've done everything correctly:

a. Place the fabric *right side up* on the *back side* of the paper foundation.

b. Cover Section 1 on the paper with fabric Piece 1. If you are not using transparent paper-piecing paper, hold your paper up to a light to check for coverage. Fabric Piece 1 should completely cover Section 1 on the pattern piece with at least ¼″ excess on all sides.

c. Glue or pin the fabric to the pattern. (If you use pins, be sure the pins don't cross the seamline between Sections 1 and 2.)

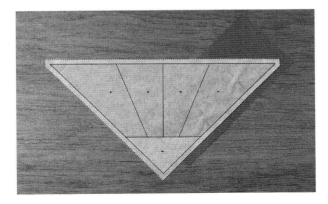

After you've placed Piece 1, you're ready to start the paper-piecing sequence.

2. Trim the fabric

Place the printed foundation paper with the fabric side down on the cutting mat. Be careful not to fold any of the fabric in the process. I like to place the pattern with the seamline I am about to sew along perpendicular to me.

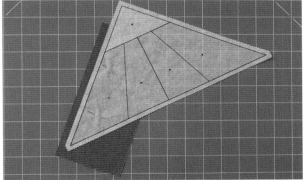

Place a thin piece of cardboard along the seamline you are about to sew along (see Block Anatomy, page 12).

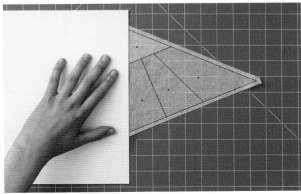

Fold the paper, but not the fabric, back along the cardboard.

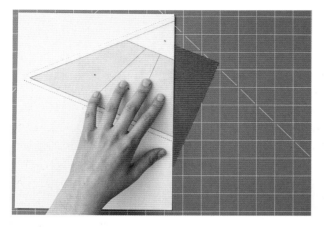

Place an Add-A-Quarter ruler along the cardboard and folded paper. Use your rotary cutter to trim along the edge of the ruler. If you don't have an Add-A-Quarter ruler as shown (below), use a clear acrylic rotary-cutting ruler to cut ¼″ away from the folded paper.

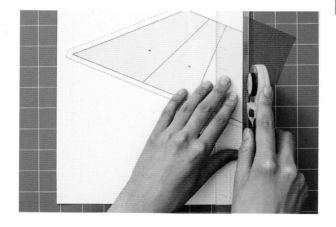

3. Place the next piece

Place the next piece right side down along the freshly trimmed fabric piece, carefully lining up the edges (the fabric should be right sides together). Make sure the fabric will extend at least ¼″ to the left and right of the intended location after it is sewn and pressed open. If you aren't using transparent paper-piecing paper, hold the pattern up to a light to check the placement. Refer to Placing Tricky Pieces (next page) to see if you need to take special care.

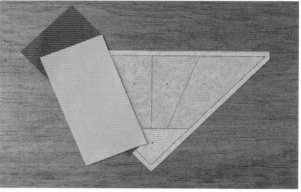

TIP

If you are crossing another seam, some fabric will "stick" to the pattern piece when you fold it back over the cardboard. Gently pull the seam away from the paper (some of the paper pattern piece will rip) until it lies flat on the mat.

Placing Tricky Pieces

JUTTING CORNERS

Sometimes the intended location for your next piece will have a corner that juts out. Make sure to place the fabric so that it extends at least ¼″ *beyond the jutting corner*—not just the seamline you are sewing along. If you place your fabric piece to extend ¼″ beyond the edge of only the seamline, it will not completely cover the intended location when you press it open.

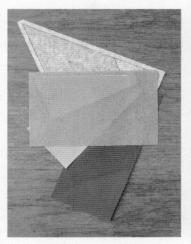 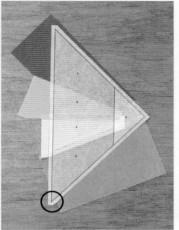

Here the fabric goes well beyond the edge of the seamline I was sewing on.

However, it did not extend beyond the jutting corner, so when I pressed it open, I didn't have enough coverage.

Double-check to make sure the fabric coverage is adequate on the other end of the seam as well. Now, when you press it open, that pesky corner should be completely covered.

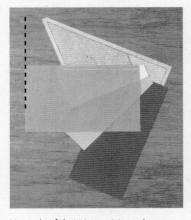 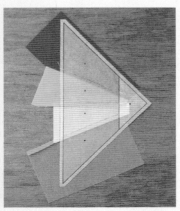

Here the fabric is positioned to cover that jutting corner.

Success!

EXTREME ANGLES

Sometimes the piece you are attaching will be at an extreme angle. Simply sewing ¼″ past the end of the seamline will not make the stitching extend all the way to the end of the next seam's allowance. If you desire, you can sew farther past the end of the seamline in order to reach the edge of the seam allowance. Some of the pieces will seem very long because the cutting directions provide enough wiggle room to do this. If you don't want to sew that far, I suggest backstitching for extra security.

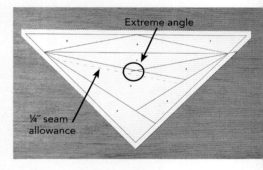

Extreme angle

¼″ seam allowance

4. Pin along the seam

You can use several options for pinning along your seams.

Pinning option 1 Place pins on the fabric side. As you sew, gently lift up the foundation paper on the side to pull them out before you reach them.

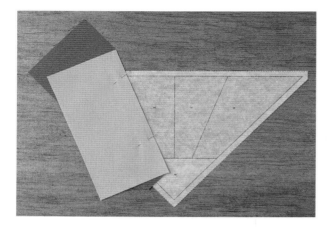

Pinning option 2 Carefully hold the fabric to the foundation paper, flip over the paper, and pin through the top of the paper. Double-check to see that the fabric is still placed correctly and hasn't bunched or shifted.

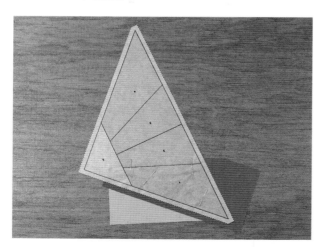

No-pinning option Sewing without using any pins is also an option. Very carefully flip over the foundation paper and move it to the sewing machine. I like to lift up the edge of the pattern in front of the sewing foot to see that the fabric pieces are still lined up. This method can save time, but it's easy for fabric to shift and pucker. When you are just starting out, it's best to pin.

TIP

Are rippling fabrics a problem? I've noticed that thinner fabrics (such as delicate shot cottons) ripple more often than thicker fabrics (such as linen) when paper piecing, and that some fabric/paper combinations cause more rippling. If you sew a seam and end up with some rippling, try firmly pressing the fabric open. You may be able to press out the ripples. If not, you'll have to rip the seam out. In the future, use more pins to help prevent additional rippling.

5. Sew along the seamline

Start about ¼" before the beginning of the seamline. Stitch along the seamline to about ¼" beyond the end of the seamline. I like to backstitch at both the beginning and end of the seamline, since ripping off foundation paper can pull stitches up at the ends of seams.

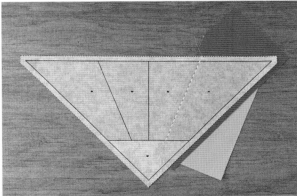

TIP

When sewing on paper foundations, you do not need the seam allowance to be on the right side of the needle because you are sewing on a line. Instead, put the smallest part of the piece you are sewing to the right of the needle. This will make it easier to sew.

TIP: Ripping Out Stitches

Mistakes happen. As with any other seam you need to rip out, just use a seam ripper or a small pair of snipping scissors to cut stitches. I prefer doing this on the fabric side of the paper-pieced unit. After you're done, gently pull off the top piece of fabric. If part of the pattern piece rips, simply place tape over the ripped area and resew.

6. Press

Press the seam. The seam allowance will end up pressed to the side underneath.

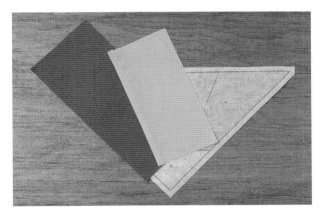

7. Add the remaining pieces

Repeat Steps 2–6 until all the pieces are attached.

TIP: Speeding Up the Process

Moving between your three paper-piecing work areas adds time to the sewing process. I like to make paper piecing more efficient by working on four blocks at a time. After I've practiced the block enough that I feel confident in it, I place and trim down each Piece 1 and position Piece 2 for four blocks. Then I sew all four of them. Finally, I press all four of them and repeat. This cuts down on the number of times I have to move from one station to another.

Trimming Down the Completed Blocks

When your blocks or units are completely sewn, you'll have a funny-looking product with strange shapes of fabric hanging off the paper on all sides. Now it's time to trim down your block: Place the completed piece, fabric side down, on your cutting mat. Use a rotary-cutting ruler to trim along the dotted lines on all sides.

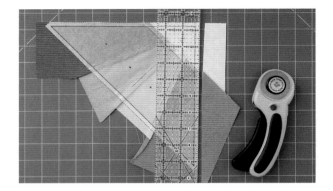

Joining Blocks and Ripping Off Papers

When your paper-pieced blocks or units are done, follow the specific project instructions to piece them together to make the quilt top. Sometimes you'll piece two paper-pieced units together; sometimes you'll stitch them to a plain piece of fabric. Either way, you'll have to decide if you want to rip off the foundation papers before or after joining the blocks. Here are your options:

Leave on the papers until after you're done piecing the area surrounding the block.   If your paper foundation extends to the very edge of the blocks, then waiting to remove the papers can help stabilize bias edges so your blocks don't stretch. You can stitch along the edge line of the block when joining pieces, stitching through the papers. If you trimmed your foundation papers down completely before you began piecing, you can sew just next to the paper, giving a scant ¼″ seam. One downside to this option is it can be more cumbersome to remove the papers at this stage because you are wrangling a large project.

Remove the papers before joining the blocks.   By removing the paper as you go, it won't be a big chore to remove all the papers at the end of the project. You also won't have to bunch up a quilt top to reach the paper on a block in the middle of the quilt. Simply remove the paper and then continue piecing as instructed, treating it as a normal quilt block. You won't need to worry about paper ending up in the seam allowances, but you do need to be very careful, as most of the edges of these paper-pieced blocks are on the bias. Use lots of pins when joining blocks because the edges will stretch easily.

I don't have a personal favorite and tend to try a few options with each quilt to see what works best. For example, I removed the papers before joining the blocks in *Diamonds and Emeralds I* (page 24), but I left them on until I pieced the entire quilt top for *Faceted Jewels I* (page 88). Whatever works for you is fine.

Matching Points When Joining Together Blocks

Because one of the goals of paper piecing is accuracy, it's important to continue being accurate when you put together the blocks.

1. Starting from the wrong side, poke a pin through the top block at the point you are looking to match. Then push the pin through the bottom block at that point, starting from the right side.

2. Use your fingers to align the 2 blocks by making the pin perpendicular to the fabric.

3. Pin the blocks together on either side of the vertical pin; *then* remove the vertical pin before sewing.

TIP: Using Directional Fabrics

If you're using a directional fabric, you may have a specific direction you want the pattern to run. Here are some tips:

1. Use tracing paper to create a cutting template that is *¾˝ larger* than the intended location for your fabric.

2. Place the fabric you are cutting *right side down* and the template you made *right side up* on top of it. (You will need to cut out the mirror image of those pieces because you piece on the back side of the pattern.)

3. Trace the cutting template onto your fabric and cut it out.

4. Carefully place the cut fabric piece along the freshly cut seam allowance of your paper-pieced pattern. Gently open the fabric to make sure it will end up covering the intended location.

5. When you are confident in the fabric placement, sew as usual.

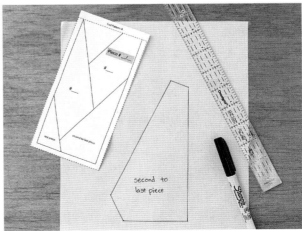

FINISHING YOUR QUILTS

Backing

All the projects in this book list the finished sizes needed for the quilt backings, so you can use your own creative license to come up with that size. Then, create a quilt sandwich by laying out your backing fabric, facedown, on a smooth surface. If possible, tape down the edges. Baste using your preferred method.

Quilting

For every project, I've discussed some different quilting ideas. You can use a simple quilting pattern, which will complement your design and act mainly as a mechanism to hold all the layers of your quilt together. Or, you can make the quilting a major element of your design, which will attract the attention of the viewer just as much as the pieced top itself. Some of your quilting decisions will depend on your quilting capabilities (or whether you want to send it out to be quilted), the amount of time you have available, and what look you are going for with your quilt. Many different quilting styles will work well with every quilt, so as long as it's something you like, it's the perfect choice. See Quilting Resources (page 111).

Sending Out Your Quilt

You may want to send out your quilts to have them quilted. This is a great option if you are working on an especially large project that would be difficult to wrangle through the throat of a domestic sewing machine, if you are particularly stumped on what quilting design to use, or if you would just prefer to have an expert work on your quilt. I used to think that having someone else quilt my projects was cheating, but I've come to love the collaboration. A good longarm quilter can turn your quilt into a beautiful piece of art. If you love completing every step of the quilting project, that's great. But if you would like to send your project to a longarm quilter, don't feel guilty about it. I'm sure you'll love the results.

I sought the help of two quilters for the projects in this book:

- Angela Walters (quiltingismytherapy.com) quilted *Icy Waters* (page 54) and *Tied Down* (page 80).

- Emily Sessions (emersonquilting.com) quilted *Apple Stars* (page 46), *The Bachelor* (page 66), *Faceted Jewels I* (page 88), and *Faceted Jewels II* (page 104).

Binding

Each project lists the yardage necessary for completing a double-fold binding using 2½˝-wide strips. To add a little something special to your quilt, you can use more than one fabric to create a scrappy binding. You may need additional yardage for some wiggle room if you choose to go this route. A number of the quilts in this book have bindings made from multiple fabrics: *Baby Jacks* (page 50), *Icy Waters* (page 54), *Tied Down* (page 80), and *Faceted Jewels I* (page 88).

PROJECTS

DIAMONDS AND EMERALDS I

This quilt with jumbo-sized blocks is perfect for beginning quilters and shows off large-scale prints beautifully. This design lends itself well to nearly any color scheme and sews up very quickly.

Materials

Using a single line of fabric is a way to easily achieve a cohesive look to your quilt. My version is made with the line Lottie Da by Heather Bailey for FreeSpirit Fabrics. This line has small-, medium-, and large-scale prints, all of which are shown off well in the large blocks. I paired these fabrics with a white-on-cream striped fabric for the background color. This subtle print added a bit of texture and interest to the quilt, while still acting as quiet space.

White: 3 yards (for background)

Prints: 16 fat quarters (for scrappy version: 64 rectangles 6″ × 7½″ and 16 rectangles 5½″ × 8½″)

Backing: 72″ × 72″

Batting: 72″ × 72″

Binding: ⅝ yard (for 2½″-wide binding strips)

Fabric labels or your favorite fabric-marking tool

Patterns: Make 64 copies of the *Diamonds and Emeralds I* pattern (pullout page P1) on your favorite 8½″ × 11″ paper-piecing paper.

Cutting Directions

WOF = width of fabric

All the fabric pieces are assigned a number (to coordinate with the order in which they are used on the pattern piece). As you cut out the fabric pieces, label each piece with the number indicated. Keep them in piles organized by their labels.

WHITE (BACKGROUND):

- Cut 16 strips 5″ × WOF. Subcut each strip into 8 squares 5″ × 5″. Subcut these squares into "stubbed" triangles (Pieces 2–5).

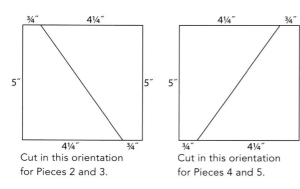

Cut in this orientation for Pieces 2 and 3.

Cut in this orientation for Pieces 4 and 5.

If using prints (or any fabric with only one right side), subcut half of the squares in one orientation and the other half in the opposite orientation.

- Cut 4 strips 5½″ × WOF.

Subcut 3 strips into 4 rectangles 5½″ × 8½″ (Piece 7).

Subcut 1 strip into 8 rectangles 5½″ × 4½″ (Piece 8).

PRINTS:

Use the cutting guide (below) to cut the following from each fat quarter:

- Cut 4 rectangles 6″ × 7½″ (Piece 1). (*Note:* If you are using a directional print, such as stripes, cut these pieces 6″ × 8½″.)

- Cut 1 rectangle 5½″ × 8½″ (Piece 6).

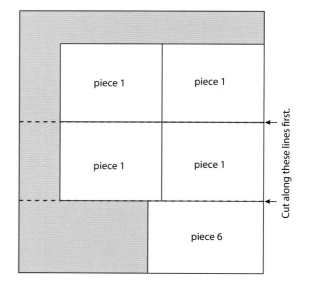

Quilt Top Construction

PAPER-PIECING ASSEMBLY

Sew each printed paper-piecing pattern. Begin with Piece 1 and work your way through Piece 5 on each pattern. Press each piece open after it is pieced. Refer to Paper-Piecing Basics (page 12) as needed.

Tricky Pieces

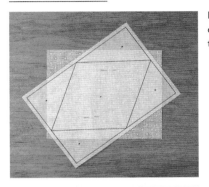

Place fabric Piece 1 diagonally to cover the diamond.

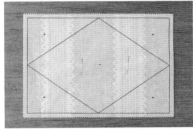

If you used directional fabrics and opted to cut your fabrics larger for the diamonds, you will place fabric Piece 1 as shown (at left).

Pieces 2–5 are stubbed triangles. This makes it easier to work with and place these fabric pieces correctly, but their orientation matters. The stubbed corners should be placed toward the middle of the pattern.

LAYOUT AND FINAL ASSEMBLY

1. Using the quilt assembly diagram (below) as a guide, arrange your quilt pieces (paper-pieced blocks and Pieces 6, 7, and 8) in a pleasing configuration. A design wall, if available, is helpful in choosing an arrangement.

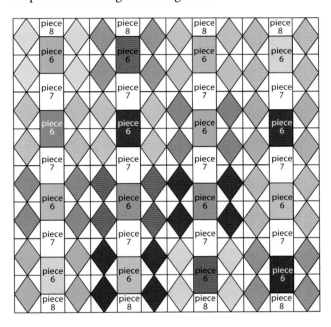

2. Piece columns of diamonds and columns of emeralds, pressing the seams open. Use the diagram to determine the exact placement of these pieces.

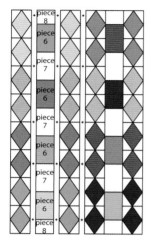

3. Sew each column, and then sew the columns together in groups of 3. Finally, sew these groups together. (Piecing the strips together in groups will reduce the need to maneuver large pieces through your machine.)

Diamonds and Emeralds I, 64˝ × 64˝, pieced by Amy Garro and Helen Kleczynski; quilted by Amy Garro

Diamonds and Emeralds I: Madrona Road (alternate colorway)

Finishing the Quilt

Baste, quilt, and bind using your favorite methods. Refer to Finishing Your Quilts (page 22) as needed.

SUGGESTED QUILTING OPTIONS

This beginning quilt is the perfect opportunity to practice your free-motion quilting skills. A simple allover pattern looks great with the large-scale blocks. Angular quilting, such as a rectangular meander, goes well with the angular blocks in this quilt. On the opposite end of the spectrum, a curvy floral quilting pattern would mimic the curvy floral patterns in the fabrics.

I decided to go for a custom look and quilted feathers creeping up and down the columns of rectangles. A dense meander in the areas between the feathers and ¼″ straight-line quilting on the outside of the two outer feathers really made the columns themselves pop. This variety of quilting patterns provides a great texture, helped by the high loft of the Hobbs wool batting I used. I quilted the *Madrona Road* version with an allover rectangular meander.

DIAMONDS AND EMERALDS II

Looking for a vivid take on *Diamonds and Emeralds I* (page 24)? This version almost shimmers with the subtle color variations and increased negative space that pops against the dark background.

Materials

I chose easy-to-read, bright, and graphic modern prints to go with this bold and graphic quilt pattern. The Mirror Ball Dots fabric gave the quilt more interest than a solid black background would have given; since the diamonds were made from either solids or text fabrics with bright backgrounds, the edges of the diamonds are still quite easy to read. I opted to use a rare Japanese text fabric for the green and yellow fabrics, but I filled in with some solid green since I had very little available. Just use a color card to match the background of the print with a solid quilting cotton fabric to keep your fabrics looking cohesive.

Black: 5¼ yards (for background)

Yellow: ½ yard (for 3 rectangles and 12 diamonds)

Green: 1 yard (for 19 rectangles and 44 diamonds)

Bright blue: ½ yard (for 2 rectangles and 13 diamonds)

Blue: 1⅝ yards (for 27 rectangles and 91 diamonds)

Backing: 72˝ × 72˝

Batting: 72˝ × 72˝

Binding: ⅝ yard (for 2½˝-wide binding strips)

Fabric labels or your favorite fabric-marking pen

Patterns: Make 160 copies of the *Diamonds and Emeralds II* pattern (pullout page P1) on your favorite 8½˝ × 11˝ paper-piecing paper.

Cutting Directions

WOF = width of fabric

All the fabric pieces are assigned a number or letter (to coordinate with the order in which they are used on the pattern piece). As you cut out the fabric pieces, label each piece with the number or letter indicated. Keep them in piles organized by their labels.

BLACK (BACKGROUND):

- Cut 27 strips 4¼″ × WOF.

  Subcut 1 strip into 8 rectangles 4¼″ × 3¼″.

  Subcut 26 strips, each into 12 rectangles 4¼″ × 3¼″; then subcut each rectangle into "stubbed" triangles, as shown (Pieces 2–5).

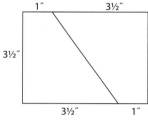

Cut in this orientation for Pieces 2 and 3.

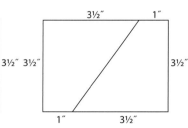

Cut in this orientation for Pieces 4 and 5.

If using prints (or any other fabric with only one right side), subcut half of the squares in one orientation for Pieces 2 and 3 and the other half in the opposite orientation for Pieces 4 and 5.

- Cut 7 strips 3¼″ × WOF.

  Subcut 1 strip into 1 rectangle 3¼″ × 36½″ (Piece Z).

  Subcut 1 strip into 1 rectangle 3¼″ × 32½″ (Piece T). Subcut the remaining fabric from this strip into 1 rectangle 3″ × 4½″.

  Subcut 1 strip into 1 rectangle 3¼″ × 20½″ (Piece U) and 1 rectangle 3¼″ × 16½″ (Piece N).

  Subcut 1 strip into 1 rectangle 3¼″ × 20½″ (Piece P) and 2 rectangles 3¼″ × 8½″ (Pieces O and W).

Subcut 1 strip into 3 rectangles 3¼″ × 8½″ (Pieces F, G, and I) and 1 rectangle 3¼″ × 4½″ (Piece C).

Subcut 2 strips, each into 3 rectangles 3¼″ × 12½″ (Pieces E, J, K, M, Q, V).

- Cut 3 strips 4½″ × WOF. Subcut each strip into 12 rectangles 4½″ × 3¼″ (Piece C).

- Cut 9 strips 3″ × WOF.

  Subcut 1 strip into 1 rectangle 3″ × 28½″ (Piece Y) and 1 rectangle 3″ × 10½″ (Piece X).

  Subcut 1 strip into 1 rectangle 3″ × 26½″ (Piece R) and 1 rectangle 3″ × 10½″ (Piece H).

  Subcut 1 strip into 1 rectangle 3″ × 26½″ (Piece L) and 1 rectangle 3″ × 12½″ (Piece S).

  Subcut 1 strip into 1 rectangle 3″ × 10½″ (Piece D) and 11 rectangles 3″ × 2½″ (Piece A).

  Subcut 5 strips, each into 8 rectangles 3″ × 4½″ (Piece B).

YELLOW:

- Cut 2 strips 3¾″ wide. Subcut each strip into 6 rectangles 3¾″ × 5″ (Piece 1).

- Cut 1 strip 3″ × WOF. Subcut into 3 rectangles 3″ × 4½″ (Piece 6).

GREEN:

- Cut 6 strips 3¾″ × WOF.

  Subcut 1 strip into 4 rectangles 3¾″ × 5″ (Piece 1).

  Subcut 5 strips into 8 rectangles 3¾″ × 5″ (Piece 1).

- Cut 2 strips 4½″ × WOF.

  Subcut 1 strip into 13 rectangles 4½″ × 3″ (Piece 6).

  Subcut 1 strip into 6 rectangles 4½″ × 3″ (Piece 6).

BRIGHT BLUE:

- Cut 2 strips 3¾″ × WOF.

  Subcut 1 strip into 8 rectangles 3¾″ × 5″ (Piece 1).

  Subcut 1 strip into 5 rectangles 3¾″ × 5″ (Piece 1) and 2 rectangles 3″ × 4½″ (Piece 6).

BLUE:

- Cut 3 strips 4½″ × WOF.

  Subcut 2 strips into 13 rectangles 4½″ × 3″ (Piece 6).

  Subcut 1 strip into 1 rectangle 4½″ × 3″ (Piece 6). Cut the remainder of this strip into 3 rectangles 3¾″ × 5″ (Piece 1).

- Cut 11 strips 3¾″ × WOF. Subcut each strip into 8 rectangles 3¾″ × 5″ (Piece 1).

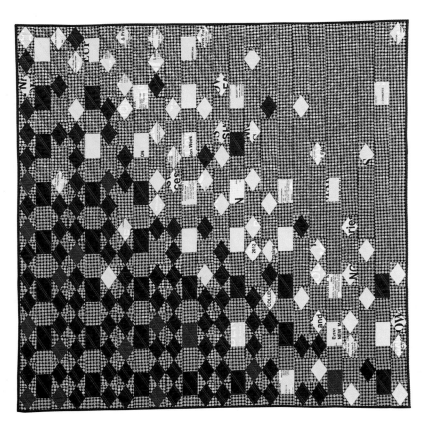

Diamonds and Emeralds II,
64″ × 64″, pieced by Lisa Parker, Holly King, and Amy Garro; quilted by Amy Garro

Quilt Top Construction

PAPER-PIECING ASSEMBLY

Work your way through the 160 paper-pieced diamonds. Begin with Piece 1 and work your way through Piece 5 on each pattern. Press each piece open after it is pieced. Refer to Paper-Piecing Basics (page 12) as needed. As you complete the diamonds, organize them into piles by color.

LAYOUT AND FINAL ASSEMBLY

1. Assemble each column as shown in the diagram (below). Be sure to use a scant ¼″ seam allowance to avoid cutting the points off of your diamonds. Press seams open when piecing together diamonds. When piecing together areas with negative space (Pieces A–Z), press toward the black fabric.

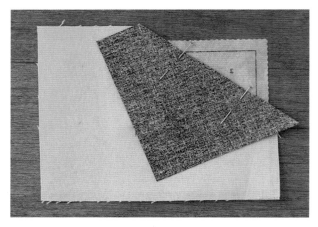

Pieces 2–5 are stubbed triangles. This makes it easier to work with and place these fabric pieces correctly, but their orientation matters. The stubbed corners should be placed toward the middle of the pattern.

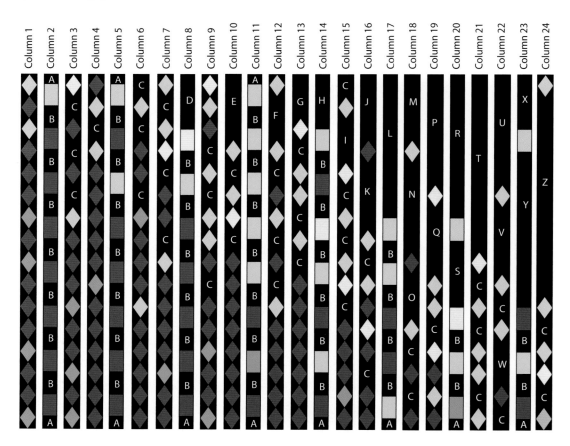

For each column, you'll need the following pieces:

COLUMN	SHAPE	PIECES
1	Diamonds	4 bright blue, 10 blue, 2 green
2	Rectangles	7 blue, 1 green, 2 Pieces A, 7 Pieces B
3	Diamonds	3 bright blue, 8 blue, 1 yellow, 1 green, 3 Pieces C
4	Diamonds	1 bright blue, 12 blue, 2 green, 1 Piece C
5	Rectangles	6 blue, 2 green, 2 Pieces A, 7 Pieces B
6	Diamonds	1 bright blue, 10 blue, 2 green, 3 Pieces C
7	Diamonds	1 bright blue, 8 blue, 1 yellow, 3 green, 3 Pieces C
8	Rectangles	5 blue, 1 yellow, 1 green, 1 Piece A, 6 Pieces B, 1 Piece D
9	Diamonds	2 bright blue, 6 blue, 1 yellow, 4 green, 3 Pieces C
10	Diamonds	8 blue, 1 yellow, 2 green, 2 Pieces C, 1 Piece E
11	Rectangles	1 bright blue, 2 blue, 5 green, 2 Pieces A, 7 Pieces B
12	Diamonds	7 blue, 4 green, 3 Pieces C, 1 Piece F
13	Diamonds	7 blue, 1 yellow, 3 green, 3 Pieces C, 1 Piece G
14	Rectangles	3 blue, 1 yellow, 3 green, 1 Piece A, 6 Pieces B, 1 Piece H
15	Diamonds	1 bright blue, 4 blue, 2 yellow, 3 green, 4 Pieces C, 1 Piece I
16	Diamonds	5 blue, 1 yellow, 2 green, 2 Pieces C, 1 Piece J, 1 Piece K
17	Rectangles	2 blue, 3 green, 1 Piece A, 4 Pieces B, 1 Piece L
18	Diamonds	3 blue, 2 green, 2 Pieces C, 1 Piece M, 1 Piece N, 1 Piece O
19	Diamonds	2 blue, 2 yellow, 3 green, 1 Piece C, 1 Piece P, 1 Piece Q
20	Rectangles	1 bright blue, 1 yellow, 2 green, 1 Piece A, 2 Pieces B, 1 Piece R, 1 Piece S
21	Diamonds	1 yellow, 4 green, 3 Pieces C, 1 Piece T
22	Diamonds	1 blue, 3 green, 2 Pieces C, 1 Piece U, 1 Piece V, 1 Piece W
23	Rectangles	2 blue, 2 green, 1 Piece A, 2 Pieces B, 1 Piece X, 1 Piece Y
24	Diamonds	1 yellow, 4 green, 2 Pieces C, 1 Piece Z

With the metallic sheen of the Mirror Ball Dots fabric, I couldn't resist using metallic silver thread.

2. Sew the columns together. Press the seams open.

TIP

Sewing a large number of long strips together can cause drifting and curving. To combat both of these problems, sew each seam in the opposite direction. Good pinning will also prevent excessive shifting.

Finishing the Quilt

Baste, quilt, and bind using your favorite methods. Refer to Finishing Your Quilts (page 22) as needed.

SUGGESTED QUILTING OPTIONS

Since this quilt is rather busy, I went with simple straight-line quilting that matched the angle of the edges of the diamonds. With the metallic sheen of the Mirror Ball Dots fabric, I couldn't resist using metallic silver thread. Evenly spaced lines seemed too simple, but I didn't think random straight lines fit the vibe of this quilt; instead, I alternated ⅜"- and 2"-wide spaces between the quilting lines.

Here are a few more quilting ideas for this project:

- Use an interlocking diamond or argyle pattern to play off of the huge pile of diamonds in this quilt.

- Add interest to your straight-line quilting by using a zigzag specialty stitch (sometimes called a honeycomb stitch) with your walking foot.

- Using thread that matches the diamond colors, quilt swirls across the quilt, changing from one thread color to another to draw the viewer's attention to the ombré effect.

- Quilt only the black areas of the quilt top with a thread that blends in, leaving the diamonds and emeralds to pop. A thicker batting will help the unquilted areas stand out even more.

CEILING TILES

Break out your low-volume prints! This modern lap quilt is easy to make and shows off those light-colored prints beautifully. With such a simple color combination, it's easy to personalize it—just add in a pop of your favorite color for the wow factor.

Materials

I used Carolyn Friedlander's Botanics line for Robert Kaufman Fabrics for this quilt. This quilt lends itself easily to both masculine and feminine fabrics to please whomever your quilt recipient might be.

Low-volume fabrics: 9 assorted prints or solids, ¾ yard each

Dark teal: 1 yard

Light teal: 1¼ yards

Backing: 68″ × 68″

Batting: 68″ × 68″

Binding: ⅝ yard (for 2½″-wide binding strips)

Fabric labels or your favorite fabric-marking pen

Patterns: Make 36 copies each of the *Ceiling Tiles* patterns A, B, and C (pullout pages P3 and P4) on your favorite 8½″ × 11″ paper-piecing paper.

Cutting Directions

WOF = width of fabric

All the fabric pieces are assigned a number (to coordinate with the order in which they are used on the pattern piece). As you cut out the fabric pieces, label each piece with the number indicated. Keep them in piles organized by their labels.

LOW-VOLUME FABRICS:

Cut the following from each fabric:

- Cut 1 strip 5¼″ × WOF. Subcut into 4 rectangles 5¼″ × 7¾″ (Piece A1).

- Cut 1 strip 5¼″ × WOF. Subcut into 8 rectangles 5¼″ × 4″ (4 Pieces B1, 4 Pieces C2).

- Cut 1 strip 5¼″ × WOF. Subcut into 4 rectangles 5¼″ × 8¼″ (Piece C3).

- Cut 1 strip 4¼″ × WOF. Subcut into 8 squares 4¼″ × 4¼″ (Piece D).

DARK TEAL:

- Cut 13 strips 2½″ × WOF.

    Subcut 2 strips into 16 squares 2½″ × 2½″ (Piece C1).

Subcut 1 strip into 4 squares 2½″ × 2½″ (Piece C1) and 2 rectangles 2½″ × 5½″ (Piece A2).

Subcut 10 strips into 7 rectangles 2½″ × 5½″ (34 Pieces A2 and 36 Pieces B2).

LIGHT TEAL:

- Cut 8 strips 3″ × WOF.

Subcut 7 strips, each into 5 rectangles 3″ × 8″ (Piece C5).

Subcut 1 strip into 1 rectangle 3″ × 8″ (Piece C5).

- Cut 6 strips 2½″ × WOF. Subcut each strip into 6 rectangles 2½″ × 6½″ (Piece C4).

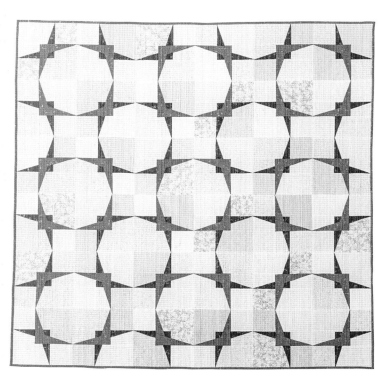

Quilt Top Construction

PAPER-PIECING ASSEMBLY

Sew each printed paper-piecing pattern. Begin with Piece 1 and work your way through the pieces numerically on each pattern. Press each piece open after it is pieced. Refer to Paper-Piecing Basics (page 12) as needed. *Note:* Pattern Piece C should be assembled with the same background fabric used for Piece C2 and Piece C3.

Tricky Pattern Pieces

Piece C2 has a long piece with an extreme *jutting corner*. You'll need to place the fabric far to the side in order to hit that corner. Piece C3 also has a jutting corner to watch out for. For both pieces, follow the directions in Jutting Corners (page 17) to place your fabric correctly.

BLOCK ASSEMBLY

For each block, you will need the following pieces:

- 1 assembled Pattern Piece A and 1 assembled Pattern Piece B, made with the same background fabric

- 1 assembled Pattern Piece C with a different background color from Pattern Pieces A and B

- 2 Pieces D cut from the same fabric but a different fabric from Pieces A, B, and C

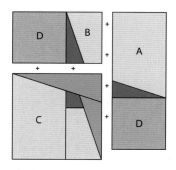

Block assembly

Ceiling Tiles, 60″ × 60″,
Pieced and quilted by Amy Garro

1. Sew together 1 Pattern Piece A and 1 Piece D. Press the seams toward Piece D.

2. Sew together 1 Pattern Piece B and 1 Piece D. Press the seams toward Piece D.

3. Sew Section BD to Piece C. Press the seams toward Piece C (or press them open, if preferred).

4. Sew Section AD to the rest of block. Press the seams toward Piece C (or press them open, if preferred).

As you assemble the blocks, sort them into stacks, keeping the same fabrics together.

LAYOUT AND FINAL ASSEMBLY

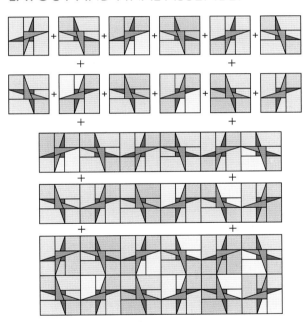

1. Lay out your block pieces into a pleasing arrangement using the quilt assembly diagram (above) for reference. Make sure the similar background fabrics aren't clumped together before you continue.

2. When satisfied with your arrangement, sew together 6 blocks to form a row. Make 6 rows total.

3. Sew the rows together.

Finishing the Quilt

Baste, quilt, and bind using your favorite methods. Refer to Finishing Your Quilts (page 22) as needed.

SUGGESTED QUILTING OPTIONS

I decided to take advantage of the low-volume fabrics in this project to play around with fun thread colors and thicknesses. I densely quilted straight lines using 40-weight rayon, 30-weight cotton, and some specialty gold thread. I think the texture is delightful. To keep the quilt from stiffening up due to the dense quilting, I used a wool batting that maintains drape even when heavily quilted.

SQUAREBURST

This simple and bright quilt makes a fun throw or picnic quilt. It's the perfect starter project for the beginning paper piecer. Half the blocks are pieced very simply in a traditional manner, which cuts down on the time spent paper piecing.

Materials

I used a variety of blenders from Michael Miller Fabrics for this quilt. By limiting each print to one or two colors plus white, it was easy to combine so many fabrics. The Happy Tones floral fabric was my starting point for choosing this color palette.

White: 1¾ yards (for background)

Prints: 13 prints, ⅝ yard each

Backing: 68″ × 68″

Batting: 68″ × 68″

Binding: ⅝ yard (for 2½″-wide binding strips)

Fabric labels or your favorite fabric-marking pen

Patterns: Make 52 copies of the *Squareburst* pattern (pullout page P2) on your favorite 8½″ × 11″ paper-piecing paper.

TIP: Trying to Go Scrappy?

From an assortment of prints, cut:

52 rectangles at least 3¾″ × 8″ (Piece 1)

52 rectangles at least 3½″ × 6½″ (Piece 2)

52 rectangles at least 3¼″ × 5½″ (Piece 3)

52 rectangles at least 4½″ × 8½″ (Piece 4)

12 squares 6½″ × 6½″ (Piece 6)

Cut the white yardage as directed in the main directions, and you're all set to go.

Cutting Directions

WOF = width of fabric; LOF = length of fabric

All the fabric pieces are assigned a number (to coordinate with the order in which they are used on the pattern piece). As you cut out the fabric pieces, label each piece with the number indicated. Keep them in piles organized by their labels.

WHITE (BACKGROUND):

- Cut 4 strips 3½″ × WOF. Subcut each strip into 6 rectangles 3½″ × 6½″ (12 Pieces 7 and 12 Pieces 8).

- Cut 8 strips 3½″ × WOF. Subcut each strip into 3 rectangles 3½″ × 12½″ (12 Pieces 9 and 12 Pieces 10).

- Cut 3 strips 5″ × WOF. Subcut each strip into 8 squares 5″ × 5″.

- From the remaining fabric, cut 2 squares 5″ × 5″. Subcut both squares into HSTs (half-square triangles) by cutting each square in half diagonally (Piece 5).

PRINT FABRICS:

Cut each print fabric in the following manner. Use the cutting guide (above right) as needed.

- Cut a 6½″ × LOF strip. From this strip, cut a 6½″ × 6½″ square (Piece 6; you will have 1 extra).

- Cut 1 strip 3¾″ × WOF. Subcut into 4 rectangles 3¾″ × 8″ (Piece 1).

- Cut 1 strip 3½″ × WOF. Subcut into 4 rectangles 3½″ × 6½″ (Piece 2).

- Cut 1 strip 3¼″ × WOF. Subcut into 4 rectangles 3¼″ × 5½″ (Piece 3).

- Cut 1 strip 4½″ × WOF. Subcut into 4 rectangles 4½″ × 8″ (Piece 4).

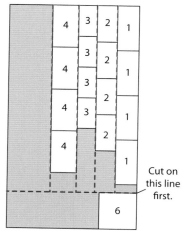

Cutting guide

Quilt Top Construction

PAPER-PIECING ASSEMBLY

Create a pile each for Pieces 1–4. Pull random fabrics from these piles as you piece the blocks to create a scrappy look. Sew 52 paper-pieced patterns.

Tricky Pattern Pieces

Section 4 on the paper-pieced pattern has a *jutting corner*. Follow the directions in Jutting Corners (page 17) to place your fabric correctly.

BLOCK ASSEMBLY

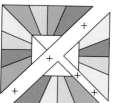

Block I construction

Block I: Piece together 4 paper-pieced triangles. Repeat to make 13 Blocks I. Press the seams open to reduce bulk.

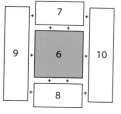

Block II construction

Block II: Sew Pieces 7 and 8 to the opposite sides of Piece 6. Press the seams open. Sew Pieces 9 and 10 to the opposite, remaining sides of Piece 6. Press seams open.

Squareburst, 60″ × 60″, pieced by Darcie Mair; quilted by Amy Garro

LAYOUT AND FINAL ASSEMBLY

1. Piece together Blocks I and II into rows as shown in the quilt layout diagram above. Press the seams toward the white sashing.

2. Finally, sew rows together (the seams will nestle where blocks meet).

Finishing the Quilt

Baste, quilt, and bind using your favorite methods. Refer to Finishing Your Quilts (page 22) as needed.

SUGGESTED QUILTING OPTIONS

Spirals centered over each block are a fun and whimsical way to break up all the straight lines of this quilt. A Baptist fan design would give a similar effect. Sometimes a very linear quilt looks good when the quilting contrasts the lines with gentle curves.

Or, in keeping with the squared look of the project, quilt meandering rectangles all over for a quick finish. You could also quilt straight lines that crosshatch across the quilt, accenting the 45° angles found in the paper-pieced blocks.

APPLE STARS

FINISHED BLOCK: 14″ × 14″

FINISHED QUILT: 50″ × 50″

Overlapping triangles create a quirky take on a traditional star pattern in this quilt. Emphasize the overall shape of the stars by making the spokes all the same color, or emphasize the way the star is created by using different fabrics for each spoke.

Materials

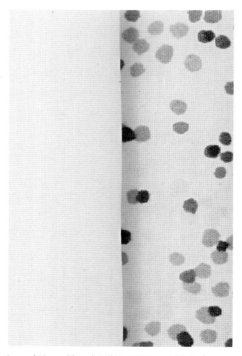

I used Kona Bleach White PFD and Melody Sketch by Nani Iro for this quilt. Melody Sketch is a double gauze fabric, which has much more stretch and shift to it than a normal quilting cotton. Paper piecing is a great way to work with these fabrics since the foundation papers act as a stabilizer. A heavy use of starch provides even more stability.

`TIP`

This print is spotted less densely along the selvages. When working with a print that does not stretch a full 40″ as you desire, be sure to order extra yardage. I ended up needing an additional yard.

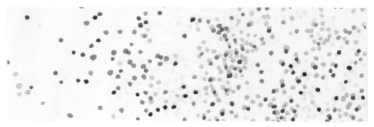

Dots: 3⅝ yards (for background)

White: 2 yards (for stars)

Backing: 58″ × 58″

Batting: 58″ × 58″

Binding: ½ yard (for 2½″-wide binding strips)

Fabric labels or your favorite fabric-marking pen

Patterns: Make 36 copies of the *Apple Stars* pattern (pullout page P1) on your favorite 8½″ × 11″ paper-piecing paper.

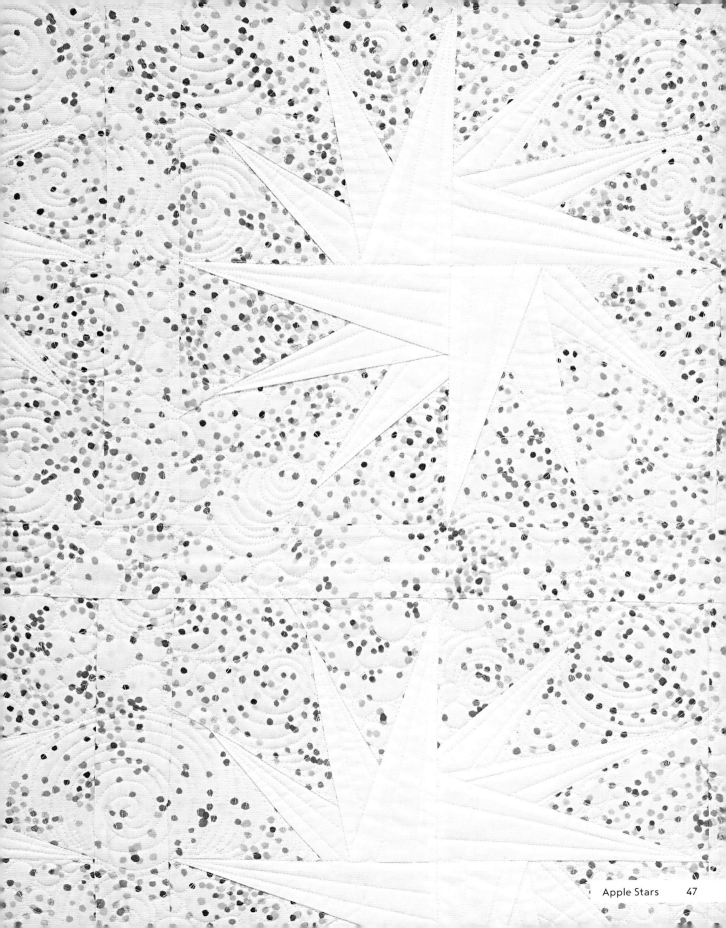

Cutting Directions

WOF = width of fabric

All the fabric pieces are assigned a number (to coordinate with the order in which they are used on the pattern piece). As you cut out the fabric pieces, label each piece with the number indicated. Keep them in piles organized by their labels.

DOTS (BACKGROUND):

- Cut 3 strips 6″ × WOF. Subcut each strip into 6 rectangles 6″ × 6½″; then subcut each rectangle into 2 triangles by cutting them in half diagonally, corner to corner (Piece 1).

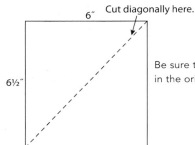

6″ Cut diagonally here.

6½″

Be sure to cut the triangles in the orientation shown.

- Cut 5 strips 8½″ × WOF. Subcut each strip into 7 rectangles 8½″ × 5½″ (Piece 3).

- Cut 6 strips 4¾″ × WOF. Subcut each strip into 6 rectangles 4¾″ × 6½″ (Piece 5).

- Cut 8 strips 2½″ × WOF. Subcut each strip into 1 rectangle 2½″ × 14½″ (Piece 7) and 1 rectangle 2½″ × 25½″ (Piece 8).

- Cut 1 strip 5½″ × WOF. Subcut into 1 rectangle 5½″ × 8½″ (Piece 3).

- From the remaining fabric, cut 2 strips 2½″ × 29″. Subcut each strip into 2 rectangles 2½″ × 14½″ to have 4 rectangles 2½″ × 14½″ (Piece 7).

WHITE (STARS):

- Cut 2 strips 7¼″ × WOF. Subcut each strip into 17 rectangles 7¼″ × 2¼″ (Piece 2).

- Cut 7 strips 2¼″ × WOF. Subcut each strip into 5 rectangles 2¼″ × 8″ (Piece 4).

- Cut 9 strips 3½″ × WOF. Subcut each strip into 4 rectangles 3½″ × 9½″ (Piece 6).

- Cut 1 strip 2¼″ × WOF. Subcut into 2 rectangles 2¼″ × 7¼″ (Piece 2) and 1 rectangle 2¼″ × 8″ (Piece 4).

Quilt Top Construction

PAPER-PIECING ASSEMBLY

Sew each printed paper-piecing pattern. Begin with Piece 1 and work your way through Piece 6 on each pattern. Refer to Paper-Piecing Basics (page 12) as needed.

Tricky Pattern Pieces

Pieces 2 and 3 on the paper-pieced patterns have *jutting corners*. Follow the directions in Jutting Corners (page 17) to place your fabric correctly.

BLOCK ASSEMBLY

Piece the blocks by sewing 2 completed paper-pieced patterns together. Piece together groups of 2 blocks. Be sure to pay attention to the orientation of your pieces as you go.

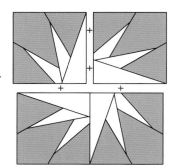

Apple Stars, 50˝ × 50˝, pieced by Amy Garro; quilted by Emily Sessions

LAYOUT AND FINAL ASSEMBLY

1. Sew a Piece 7 between a line of 3 blocks to create a row. Sew a Piece 7 to each end of the row. Repeat to create 3 rows.

2. Sew together 2 Pieces 8 to create a 50½˝ strip. Make 4. Sew the 50½˝ strips between the 3 rows. Sew a 50½˝ strip to the 2 remaining sides of the quilt top.

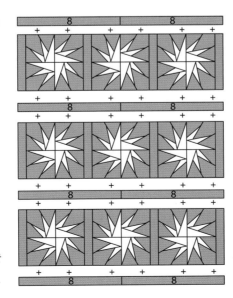

 TIP

Be careful not to blunt the corners of the stars that touch the sashing. Avoid this by using a *scant* ⅓˝ for the sashing seams.

Finishing the Quilt

Baste, quilt, and bind using your favorite methods. Refer to Finishing Your Quilts (page 22) as needed.

SUGGESTED QUILTING OPTIONS

Emily quilted straight lines in the stars, and bubbles and spirals in the background, which went well with the dotted background fabric I used. It also provides a fun feeling of a nighttime sky to the quilting pattern.

Other quilting options:

- Use a swirly Spiro graph–style quilting design in each star and a free-motion filler for the background.

- Quilt straight lines in the background, radiating out from the center of each star. Stitch in-the-ditch along the seams within the star to keep the focus on the radiating lines, while still stabilizing the rest of the block.

BABY JACKS

This version of the jumping jacks block has fewer seams to match than in *Jumping Jacks* (page 96), making it easier to construct. This pattern lends itself well to scrappy piecing, while still looking cohesive by having one color group for the jumping jacks and another for the "bow ties."

Materials

I used a variety of low-volume prints with grays and blues to create a fun baby boy quilt. Since you only need a little bit of each fabric, I was able to use up a lot of smaller scraps from my stash on this project.

Whites: 9 assorted prints, ¼ yard each

Blues: 9 assorted prints, 1 fat eighth of each

Grays: 6 assorted prints, 1 fat eighth of each

Backing: 44″ × 44″

Batting: 44″ × 44″

Binding: ½ yard (for 2½″-wide binding strips)

Fabric labels or your favorite fabric-marking pen

Patterns: Make 18 copies each of *Baby Jacks* patterns A and B (pullout pages P1 and P4) on your favorite 8½″ × 11″ paper-piecing paper.

TIP: Want to Make a Twin-Size Quilt?

This baby quilt uses 9 blocks, and a twin-size version uses 35. So multiply the yardage requirements and cutting directions by 4 if you want to make a twin. You'll end up with 36 blocks—perfect for a 5 × 7 block arrangement with an extra block for the back. The twin-size version will finish at 60″ × 84″.

Cutting Directions

WOF = width of fabric

All the fabric pieces are assigned a number (to coordinate with the order in which they are used on the pattern piece). As you cut out the fabric pieces, label each piece with the number indicated. Keep them in piles organized by their labels.

WHITE PRINTS:

From each white print:

- Cut 4 rectangles 2¾" × 7"
  (Pieces A3 and B3).

- Cut 2 rectangles 6½" × 7¼".
  Subcut each rectangle
  into 2 "stubbed" triangles,
  following the diagrams
  below (Pieces A1 and B1).
  Cut a rectangle in each
  orientation shown.

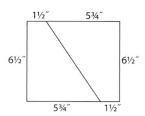

Pieces A1

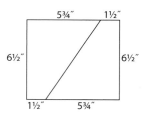

Pieces B1

BLUE PRINTS:

From each blue print:

- Cut 4 rectangles 4" × 9"
  (Pieces A2 and B2).

GRAY PRINTS:

From each gray print:

- Cut 3 rectangles 5" × 7¾"
  (Piece B4).

Quilt Top Construction

PAPER-PIECING ASSEMBLY

Sew each printed paper-piecing pattern. Begin with Piece A1 and work your way through Piece A3 and B1 through B4 on each pattern. Press each piece open after it is pieced. Refer to Paper-Piecing Basics (page 12) as needed.

Tricky Pieces

Pieces A2 and B2 have *jutting corners*. Follow the directions in Jutting Corners (page 17) to place your fabric correctly.

BLOCK ASSEMBLY

1. Arrange your block pieces into a pleasing arrangement. Make sure the prints aren't clumped together before you continue.

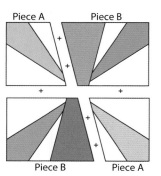

2. When satisfied with your arrangement, piece together pairs of pattern Pieces A and B in each block. These are angled seams, so you will need to take extra care when joining them (see Matching Angled Seam Pieces, below). Press toward the bow tie (Pattern Piece B).

3. Piece together each pair. Press the seams open.

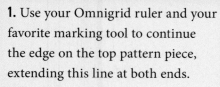

Matching Angled Seam Pieces

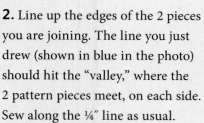

1. Use your Omnigrid ruler and your favorite marking tool to continue the edge on the top pattern piece, extending this line at both ends.

2. Line up the edges of the 2 pieces you are joining. The line you just drew (shown in blue in the photo) should hit the "valley," where the 2 pattern pieces meet, on each side. Sew along the ¼" line as usual.

Finishing the Quilt

Baste, quilt, and bind using your favorite methods. Refer to Finishing Your Quilts (page 22) as needed.

SUGGESTED QUILTING OPTIONS

I chose a different quilting design for each color group in this quilt. I used some circular stencils to create my own custom quilting stencil for the blue jacks, straight-line quilted the gray areas, and stippled the low-volume background. Since baby quilts get a lot of wear and tear, quick options with good coverage (such as a basic meander) are great. You could also add a touch of whimsy by quilting verses from your favorite nursery rhyme or baby book.

LAYOUT AND FINAL ASSEMBLY

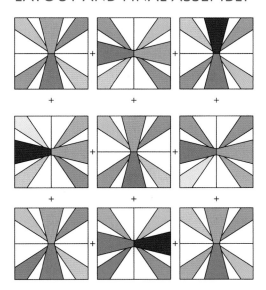

1. Sew 3 rows of 3 blocks. Press the seams open.

2. Sew together the 3 rows. Press the seams open.

Baby Jacks, 36″ × 36″, pieced and quilted by Amy Garro

ICY WATERS

All you negative-space and ombré lovers, here's your gem: a striking twin-sized quilt that would look fantastic in a modern bedroom, over the back of a sleek couch, or even as a wallhanging. Fun fact: The entire quilt is made from one block, reflected, rotated, and with different color placement to create variety.

Materials

I used a selection of Kona solids to create an ombré effect, moving from white, through some blues, to a deep purple. Moving through light tealy blues on the way to purple provided more interest and sparkle to the quilt than if I had used only blues.

Color A: Kona Regal, 1 yard

Color B: Kona Deep Blue, 1 yard

Color C: Kona Pacific, 1½ yards

Color D: Kona Lagoon, 1¼ yards

Color E: Kona Peacock, 1¾ yards

Color F: Kona Lake, 1¾ yards

White: 3½ yards

Backing: 62″ × 80″

Batting: 62″ × 80″

Binding: ⅔ yard (for 2½″-wide binding strips)

Fabric labels or your favorite fabric-marking pen

Patterns: Make 35 copies of *Icy Waters* pattern Piece A (pullout page P1) and 9 copies of *Icy Waters* pattern Piece B (pullout page P1) on your favorite 8½″ × 11″ paper-piecing paper. The pattern will use 2 pieces of paper, which you'll need to tape together with painter's or masking tape.

NOTE

The pattern pieces have dashed lines because some blocks use larger pieces of white fabric, which end up covering more than one location. In these cases, the intended combined location will be indicated with hyphens (for example, White Piece 1-2-3 is a piece of white fabric that will cover locations 1, 2, and 3, preventing the need for seams between each of these pieces). If you desire, you can use a pen to make the dashed lines on the patterns solid, leaving them dashed only when you will cover multiple locations at a time.

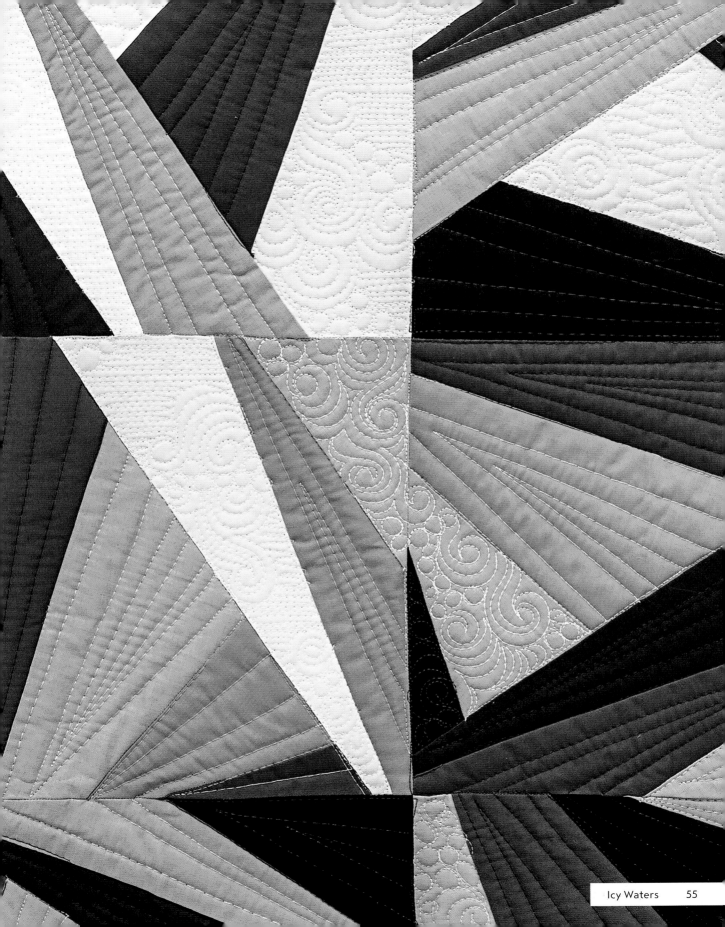

Cutting Directions

WOF = width of fabric

All the fabric pieces are assigned a number (to coordinate with the order in which they are used on the pattern piece). As you cut out the fabric pieces, label each piece with the number indicated. Keep them in piles organized by their labels.

The cutting directions given are based on using solids, which do not have a right side.

CUTTING PIECE 1 FOR ALL COLORS:

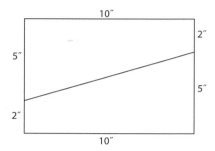

Piece 1 is a stubbed triangle. For Piece 1 of each color, subcut the stubbed triangles as shown in the cutting guide.

COLOR A (KONA REGAL):

- Cut 1 strip 7″ × WOF.

  Subcut into 1 rectangle 7″ × 10″. Subcut the rectangle into stubbed triangles using the Cutting Piece 1 directions (Piece A1).

  Trim the remaining amount of the strip to 5″ wide. Subcut into 2 rectangles 5″ × 10″ (Piece A2).

- Cut 1 strip 4″ × WOF. Subcut into 3 rectangles 4″ × 13″ (Piece A5).

- Cut 1 strip 3″ × WOF. Subcut into 3 rectangles 3″ × 11½″ (Piece A6).

- Cut 1 strip 4½″ × WOF. Subcut into 4 rectangles 4½″ × 7″ (Piece A3).

- From the remaining fabric, cut 1 rectangle 4″ × 7½″ (Piece A7) and 2 rectangles 3″ × 6″ (Piece A4).

COLOR B (KONA DEEP BLUE):

- Cut 1 strip 4″ × WOF. Subcut into 5 rectangles 4″ × 7½″ (Piece B7).

- Cut 2 strips 4″ × WOF.

  Subcut 1 strip into 3 rectangles 4″ × 13″ (Piece B5).

  Subcut 1 strip into 2 rectangles 4″ × 13″ (Piece B5).

- Cut 1 strip 5″ × WOF. Subcut into 4 rectangles 5″ × 10″ (Piece B2).

- Cut 1 strip 7″ × WOF. Subcut into 1 rectangle 7″ × 10″. Subcut each rectangle into triangles using Cutting Piece 1 directions (Piece B1).

- From the remaining fabric, cut 2 rectangles 3″ × 6″ (Piece B4), 1 rectangle 5″ × 10″ (Piece B2), and 1 rectangle 4½″ × 7″ (Piece B3).

Icy Waters, 54″ × 72″, pieced by Amy Garro; quilted by Angela Walters

COLOR C (KONA PACIFIC):

- Cut 1 strip 7″ × WOF. Subcut into 4 rectangles 7″ × 10″. Subcut each rectangle into stubbed triangles using the Cutting Piece 1 directions (Piece C1).

- Cut 2 strips 5″ × WOF.

  Subcut 1 strip into 3 rectangles 5″ × 10″ (Piece D6).

  Subcut 1 strip into 2 rectangles 5″ × 10″ (Piece C2).

- Cut 1 strip 4½″ × WOF. Subcut into 3 rectangles 4½″ × 7″ (Piece C3). From the remaining fabric, cut 1 rectangle 4″ × 13″ (Piece C5).

- Cut 5 strips 3″ × WOF.

  Subcut 1 strip into 6 rectangles 3″ × 6″ (Piece C4).

  Subcut 1 strip into 3 rectangles 3″ × 6″ (Piece C4) and 1 rectangle 3″ × 11½″ (Piece C6).

  Subcut 3 strips into 3 rectangles 3″ × 11½″ (Piece C6).

COLOR D (KONA LAGOON):

- Cut 1 strip 7″ × WOF. Subcut into 2 rectangles 7″ × 10″. Subcut each rectangle into stubbed triangles, using Cutting Piece 1 directions (Piece D1).

- Cut 1 strip 5″ × WOF. Subcut into 4 rectangles 5″ × 10″ (Piece D2).

- Cut 2 strips 3″ × WOF.

  Subcut 1 strip into 3 rectangles 3″ × 11½″ (Piece D6).

  Subcut 1 strip into 1 rectangle 3″ × 11½″ (Piece D6).

- Cut 1 strip 4″ × WOF. Subcut into 4 rectangles 4″ × 7½″ (Piece D7).

- Cut 3 strips 4½″ × WOF.

  Subcut 2 strips, each into 5 rectangles 4½″ × 7″ (Piece D3).

  Subcut 1 strip into 1 rectangle 4½″ × 7″ (Piece D3).

  From the remaining fabric, cut 1 rectangle 4″ × 13″ (Piece D5) and 3 rectangles 3″ × 6″ (Piece D4).

COLOR E (KONA PEACOCK):

- Cut 1 strip 7″ × WOF. Subcut into 3 rectangles 7″ × 10″. Subcut each rectangle into stubbed triangles, using Cutting Piece 1 directions (Piece E1).

- Cut 1 strip 5″ × WOF. Subcut into 3 rectangles 5″ × 10″ (Piece E2).

- Cut 1 strip 5″ × WOF. Subcut into 4 rectangles 5″ × 10″ (Piece E2).

- Cut 1 strip 13″ × WOF. Subcut into 10 rectangles 13″ × 4″ (Piece E5).

- Cut 2 strips 4″ × WOF. Subcut each strip into 3 rectangles 4″ × 13″ (Piece E5).

- Cut 1 strip 7½″ × WOF. Subcut into 10 rectangles 7½″ × 4″ (Piece E7).

- Cut 1 strip 3″ × WOF. Subcut into 4 rectangles 3″ × 6″ (Piece E4).

- Cut 1 strip 3″ × WOF. Subcut into 2 rectangles 3″ × 11½″ (Piece E6).

- Cut 1 strip 4½″ × WOF. Subcut into 3 rectangles 4½″ × 7″ (Piece E3).

COLOR F (KONA LAKE):

- Cut 1 strip 7″ × WOF. Subcut into 3 rectangles 7″ × 10″. Subcut each rectangle into stubbed triangles, using Cutting Piece 1 directions (Piece F1).

- Cut 3 strips 5″ × WOF.

  Subcut 2 strips into 4 rectangles 5″ × 10″ (Piece F2).

  Subcut 1 strip into 3 rectangles 5″ × 10″ (Piece F2).

- Cut 2 strips 4″ × WOF. Subcut each strip into 3 rectangles 4″ × 13″ (Piece F5).

- Cut 2 strips 3″ × WOF. Subcut each strip into 3 rectangles 3″ × 11½″ (Piece F6).

- Cut 2 strips 4″ × WOF. Subcut each strip into 5 rectangles 4″ × 7½″ (Piece F7).

- Cut 1 strip 4½″ × WOF.

  Subcut into 3 rectangles 4½″ × 7″ (Piece F3).

  From the remaining fabric, cut 1 rectangle 4″ × 7½″ (Piece F7).

- Cut 1 strip 6″ × WOF. Subcut into 9 rectangles 6″ × 3″ (Piece F4).

WHITE (KONA WHITE):

- Cut 2 strips 7″ × WOF.

  Subcut 1 strip into 4 rectangles 7″ × 10″ (Piece 1).

  Subcut 1 strip into 3 rectangles 7″ × 10″. Subcut each piece into stubbed triangles, using Cutting Piece 1 directions (Piece 1).

- Cut 1 strip 7″ × WOF. Subcut into 6 rectangles 7″ × 4½″ (Piece 3).

- Cut 1 strip 3″ × WOF. Subcut into 5 rectangles 3″ × 6″ (Piece 4).

- Cut 2 strips 4″ × WOF.

  Subcut 1 strip into 3 rectangles 4″ × 13″ (Piece 5).

  Subcut 1 strip into 1 rectangle 4″ × 13″ (Piece 5).

- Cut 1 strip 11½″ × WOF. Subcut into 11 rectangles 11½″ × 3″ (Piece 6).

- Cut 1 strip 7½″ × WOF. Subcut into 8 rectangles 7½″ × 4″ (Piece 7).

- Cut 2 strips 10″ × WOF.

  Subcut 1 strip into 2 squares 10″ × 10″ (Piece 1-2-3-4-5), 1 square 10″ × 10″ (Piece 1-2-3-4-5-6), and 1 rectangle 10″ × 8″ (Piece 2-3-4).

  Subcut 1 strip into 1 rectangle 10″ × 5″ (Piece 2), 1 rectangle 10″ × 7″ (Piece 2-3), 2 rectangles 10″ × 9½″ (Piece 1-2-3-4), and 1 rectangle 10″ × 8½″ (Piece 1-2-3).

- Cut 1 strip 10″ × WOF. Subcut into 1 rectangle 10″ × 8½″ (Piece 1-2-3); then cut the remaining strip lengthwise into 1 strip 5½″ × WOF and 1 strip 4½″ × WOF.

  From the 5½″ strip, subcut into 4 rectangles 5½″ × 6½″ (Piece 3-4).

  From the 4½″ strip, subcut into 2 rectangles 4½″ × 11½″ (Piece 6-7).

- Cut 1 strip 13″ × WOF. Subcut into 2 rectangles 13″ × 4½″ (Piece 5-6) and 3 rectangles 13″ × 7″ (Piece 5-6-7).

- From the remaining fabric, cut 1 square 18½″ × 18½″ (Block 1-2-7-8).

Quilt Top Construction

PAPER-PIECING ASSEMBLY

To help you keep track of your blocks, each pattern piece has a line on which to write the block number.

Sew each printed paper-piecing pattern. Begin with Piece 1 and work your way through Piece 7 on each pattern, referring to the block key (pages 60 and 61) to find the unique color placement for each block. The blocks in the key are shown in the same orientation to make it easier to follow along while piecing. Refer to Paper-Piecing Basics (page 12) as needed.

Tricky Pattern Pieces

Pieces 2 and 3 on the paper-pieced patterns have *jutting corners*. Follow the directions in Jutting Corners (page 17) to place your fabric correctly.

TIP

I suggest making a color copy of the key and crossing off each block as you complete it.

Block Key

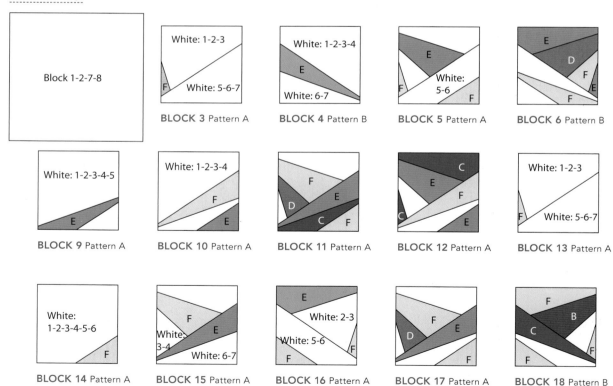

Block 1-2-7-8

White: 1-2-3 / F / White: 5-6-7
BLOCK 3 Pattern A

White: 1-2-3-4 / E / White: 6-7
BLOCK 4 Pattern B

E / F / White: 5-6 / F
BLOCK 5 Pattern A

E / D / F / E / F
BLOCK 6 Pattern B

White: 1-2-3-4-5 / E
BLOCK 9 Pattern A

White: 1-2-3-4 / F / E / E
BLOCK 10 Pattern A

F / E / D / C / F
BLOCK 11 Pattern A

C / E / F / C / E
BLOCK 12 Pattern A

White: 1-2-3 / F / White: 5-6-7
BLOCK 13 Pattern A

White: 1-2-3-4-5-6 / F
BLOCK 14 Pattern A

F / White: 3-4 / E / White: 6-7
BLOCK 15 Pattern A

E / White: 2-3 / White: 5-6 / F / F
BLOCK 16 Pattern A

E / F / D / F
BLOCK 17 Pattern A

F / B / C / F / F
BLOCK 18 Pattern B

BLOCK 19 Pattern A

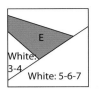

BLOCK 20 Pattern A

BLOCK 21 Pattern A

BLOCK 22 Pattern A

BLOCK 23 Pattern A

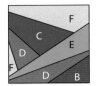

BLOCK 24 Pattern A

BLOCK 25 Pattern A

BLOCK 26 Pattern A

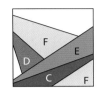

BLOCK 27 Pattern A

BLOCK 28 Pattern A

BLOCK 29 Pattern A

BLOCK 30 Pattern A

BLOCK 31 Pattern B

BLOCK 32 Pattern A

BLOCK 33 Pattern B

BLOCK 34 Pattern A

BLOCK 35 Pattern A

BLOCK 36 Pattern A

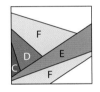

BLOCK 37 Pattern A

BLOCK 38 Pattern A

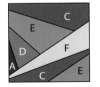

BLOCK 39 Pattern A

BLOCK 40 Pattern B

BLOCK 41 Pattern B

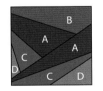

BLOCK 42 Pattern A

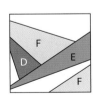

BLOCK 43 Pattern A

BLOCK 44 Pattern A

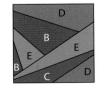

BLOCK 45 Pattern A

BLOCK 46 Pattern B

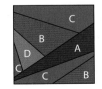

BLOCK 47 Pattern A

BLOCK 48 Pattern A

LAYOUT AND FINAL ASSEMBLY

When your blocks are done, lay them out in order. Use the row construction diagrams (below) to rotate the blocks into their correct placement.

Rows 1 and 2

1. Sew the 9″ blocks together into 2 rows. Press the seams open.

2. Sew these 2 short rows together. Press the seams open.

3. Sew the 2 short rows to Block 1-2-7-8. Press the seams open.

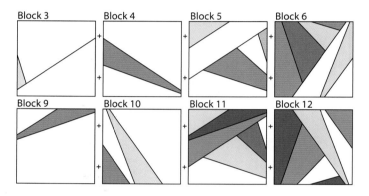

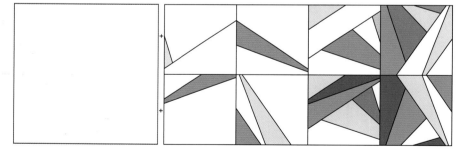

REMAINING CONSTRUCTION

1. For remaining rows, sew the 9″ blocks together into rows.

2. Sew the rows together. Press the seams open.

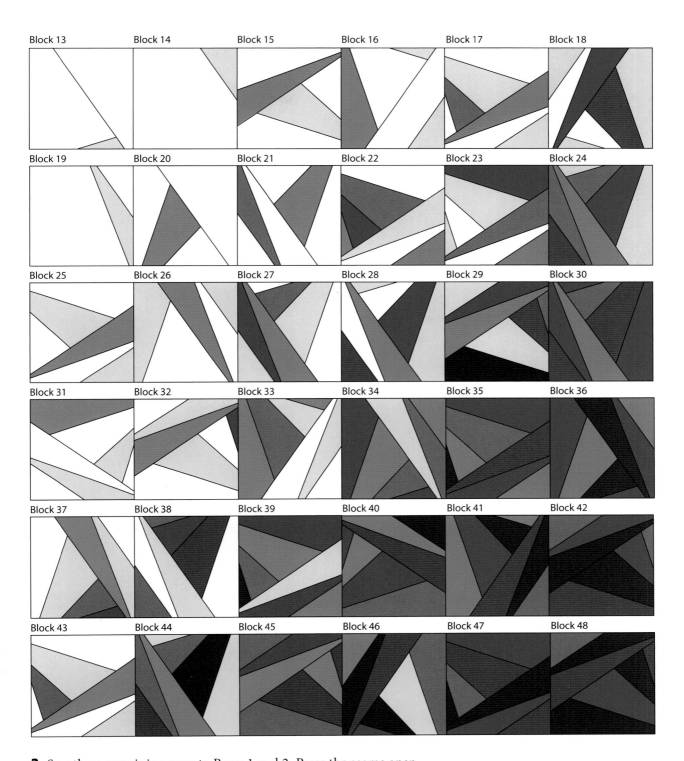

Block 13 Block 14 Block 15 Block 16 Block 17 Block 18
Block 19 Block 20 Block 21 Block 22 Block 23 Block 24
Block 25 Block 26 Block 27 Block 28 Block 29 Block 30
Block 31 Block 32 Block 33 Block 34 Block 35 Block 36
Block 37 Block 38 Block 39 Block 40 Block 41 Block 42
Block 43 Block 44 Block 45 Block 46 Block 47 Block 48

3. Sew these remaining rows to Rows 1 and 2. Press the seams open.

Finishing the Quilt

Baste, quilt, and bind using your favorite methods. Refer to Finishing Your Quilts (page 22) as needed.

SUGGESTED QUILTING OPTIONS

Angela used patterns that mimicked the movement one might see in choppy waters—ranging from shapes like swirls and pebbles to wavy lines with swoops. Shifting between these free-motion patterns emphasized the movement within the quilt pattern.

Some other quilting ideas:

* Random straight lines hitting the quilt at all different directions would fit really well with this quilt's random-seeming array of shapes and angles.

* Customized quilting will really complement the design of this quilt, but an allover pattern that is quieter and lets the pattern speak for itself will work well also. Gentle waves moving across the quilt will help give some movement without taking the focus away from the graphic impact of your project.

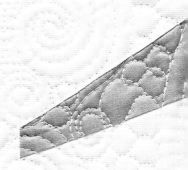

The quilting patterns mimic the movement one might see in choppy waters.

THE BACHELOR

This manly quilt is great for the bachelor in your life—perhaps a son or brother, or even a husband who might like his own quilt. Its large size accommodates a snooze on the couch for even the tallest of men. Modified Log Cabin blocks with ⅛″ details are surrounded by simple strip piecing, making this a quick quilt to pull together.

Materials

For this quilt, I chose Essex Yarn Dyed Linen in Steel and Black, Kona Poppy, Michael Miller Couture Cranberry, Kona Ruby, and Kona Crimson fabrics. I used Essex Yarn Dyed Linen for its masculine feel; it also provides some texture and subtle patterning to an area of large negative space, giving it more interest than regular quilting cotton solids. Because Essex Linen is more prone to raveling than quilting cottons, I suggest using a ½″ seam allowance and reinforcing all seams with an overlock or zigzag stitch in the seam allowance. For the paper-pieced block itself, I chose to use a ¼″ seam allowance to reduce bulk and reinforced the block by ironing fusible interfacing onto the back. If you would prefer to use ½″ seam allowances in the block, I suggest adding ½″ to each dimension of the reds included in the block. Instead of using an Add-A-Quarter ruler, use a regular Omnigrid acrylic ruler to add the ½″.

Light gray solid: Essex Yarn Dyed Linen in Steel, 1 yard

Dark gray solid: Essex Yarn Dyed Linen in Black, 7¼ yards

Light red: 1 yard

Medium red I: ⅝ yard

Medium red II: ¾ yard

Dark red: ½ yard

Backing: 88″ × 109″

Batting: 88″ × 109″

Binding: 1 yard (for 2½″-wide binding strips)

Lightweight fusible interfacing: 2 yards

Fabric labels or your favorite fabric-marking pen

Patterns: Make 5 copies of *The Bachelor* pattern (pullout page P4) on 5 pieces of 11″ × 17″ copy paper or on 10 pieces of your favorite 8½″ × 11″ paper-piecing paper. Tape together with painter's or masking tape if using 8½″ × 11″ paper. Trim as necessary.

Cutting Directions

WOF = width of fabric

All the fabric pieces are assigned a number (to coordinate with the order in which they are used on the pattern piece). As you cut out the fabric pieces, label each piece with the number indicated. Keep them in piles organized by their labels.

LIGHT GRAY:

- Cut 4 strips 3½″ × WOF. Trim to 40″ in length.

- Cut 3 strips 5″ × WOF. Trim to 40″ in length.

DARK GRAY:

- Cut 2 strips 47″ × WOF. Subcut each strip into 3 rectangles 47″ × 12″.

- Cut 7 strips 6″ × WOF. Trim to 40″ in length.

- Cut 2 strips 6½″ × WOF. Trim to 40″ in length.

- Cut 2 strips 23″ × WOF. Subcut each strip into 3 rectangles 23″ × 12″.

- Cut 1 strip 7″ × WOF. Subcut into 3 rectangles 7″ × 13″.

- Cut 1 strip 9½″ × WOF.

  Subcut 2 rectangles 9½″ × 13″.

  From the remaining fabric, cut 1 rectangle 7″ × 13″.

- Cut 25 strips 1″ × WOF.

- Cut 2 strips 1¼″ × WOF.

LIGHT RED:

- Cut 1 strip 5″ × WOF.

  Subcut into 1 rectangle 5″ × 9½″ (Piece 44).

  Trim the remaining fabric to 4″ wide. Subcut into 4 rectangles 4″ × 7″ (Piece 45).

- Cut 1 strip 5″ × WOF. Subcut into 4 rectangles 5″ × 9½″ (Piece 44).

- Cut 1 strip 13″ × WOF.

  Subcut into 5 rectangles 13″ × 6½″ (Piece 43).

- From the remaining fabric, cut 1 rectangle 4″ × 7″ (Piece 45) and 5 rectangles 2″ × 3½″ (Piece 1).

MEDIUM RED I:

- Cut 1 strip 1¾″ × WOF. Subcut into 10 rectangles 1¾″ × 4″ (Pieces 6 and 7).

- Cut 1 strip 1½″ × WOF. Subcut into 5 rectangles 1½″ × 7½″ (Piece 39).

- Cut 1 strip 3½″ × WOF. Subcut into 5 rectangles 3½″ × 1½″ (Piece 8) and 5 rectangles 3½″ × 2¾″ (Piece 9).

- Cut 4 strips 2¼″ × WOF.

  Subcut 1 strip into 3 rectangles 2¼″ × 13″ (Piece 37).

  Subcut 1 strip into 2 rectangles 2¼″ × 13″ (Piece 37) and 1 rectangle 2¼″ × 11½″ (Piece 38).

  Subcut 1 strip into 3 rectangles 2¼″ × 11½″ (Piece 38).

  Subcut 1 strip into 1 rectangle 2¼″ × 11½″ (Piece 38).

MEDIUM RED II:

- Cut 1 strip 4¼″ × WOF. Subcut into 5 squares 4¼″ × 4¼″ (Piece 17) and 5 rectangles 4½″ × 1¼″ (Piece 16).

- Cut 1 strip 14″ × WOF.

  Subcut into 10 rectangles 14″ × 2″ (Pieces 30 and 31).

  From the remaining fabric, cut 1 section 6¼″ × 17½″. Subcut into 10 rectangles 6¼″ × 1¾″ (Pieces 14 and 15).

  From the remaining fabric, cut 1 section 6¾″ × 7½″. Subcut into 5 rectangles 6¾″ × 1½″ (Piece 32).

- From the remaining fabric, cut 5 rectangles 1½″ × 2½″ (Piece 33).

DARK RED:

- Cut 1 strip 6½″ × WOF. Subcut into 5 rectangles 6½″ × 6″ (Piece 25) and 5 rectangles 6½″ × 1½″ (Piece 24).

- Cut 3 strips 2″ × WOF. Subcut into 10 rectangles 2″ × 10″ (Pieces 22 and 23).

FEATHERWEIGHT FUSIBLE INTERFACING:

- Cut 5 squares 13″ × 13″.

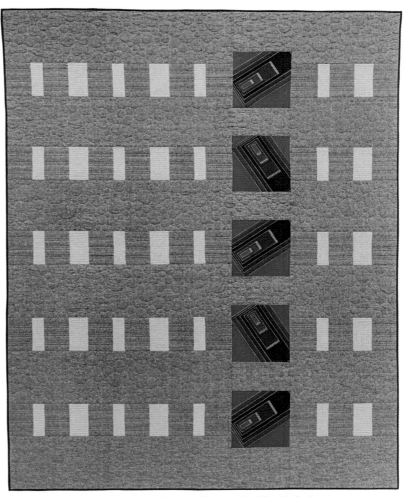

The Bachelor, 80″ × 101″, pieced by Amy Garro; quilted by Emily Sessions

Quilt Top Construction

Use a ½" seam allowance for all piecing. Reinforce seams with an overlock or zigzag stitch.

IMPORTANT NOTE: *If you use a ¼" seam, your measurements will be off!*

PAPER-PIECING ASSEMBLY

Sew each printed paper-piecing pattern. Begin with Piece 1 and work your way through Piece 45 on each pattern. Press each seam open after piecing. Refer to Paper-Piecing Basics (page 12) as needed.

NOTE

As you piece the blocks, you need to cut the 1"- and 1½"-wide gray strips to length. Simply trim off sections to the desired length as you work through piecing the blocks. When you reach the end of a fabric strip, set it aside to use for future, smaller pieces. Cut more gray strips if necessary.

If desired, iron fusible interfacing to the back of the paper-pieced blocks. Follow the manufacturer's instructions for your interfacing product. I did this to further strengthen the lines, but it isn't necessary with regular quilting cottons.

LAYOUT AND FINAL ASSEMBLY

Use a ½" seam allowance for all piecing. Reinforce seams with an overlock or zigzag stitch.

Left Section

1. Piece 5 dark gray rectangles 6" × 40", 3 light gray rectangles 3½" × 40", 2 light gray rectangles 5" × 40", and 1 dark gray rectangle 6½" × 40" together, following the diagram. Press all seams toward the dark gray fabric.

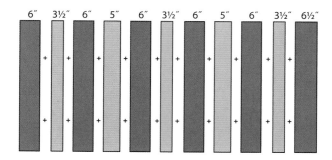

2. Subcut each section into 5 pieced strips 8″ in height.

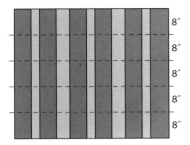

TIP

You have a few options for cutting such a large piece of fabric. You can carefully fold the fabric in half multiple times until you can rotary cut as usual, making sure that the edges all match up and the fabric is not distorted, or you can use an extra-large ruler to carefully mark a line parallel to the edge of the fabric at 8″. Omnigrid makes an 8½″ × 24″ ruler that would help you accomplish this task easily. Then cut with scissors.

3. Sew your strip-pieced sections from Step 2 between the 12″ × 47″ sections. Press toward the unpieced, dark gray fabric sections.

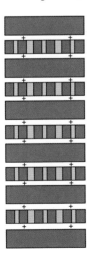

Right Section

1. Piece 2 dark gray rectangles 6″ × 40″, 1 light gray rectangle 3½″ × 40″, 1 light gray rectangle 5″ × 40″, and 1 dark gray rectangle 6½″ × 40″ as shown in the diagram. Press toward the dark gray fabric.

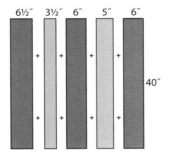

2. Subcut each section into 5 pieced strips 8″ in height.

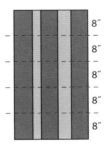

3. Sew your strip-pieced sections from Step 2 between the 12″ × 23″ sections. Press toward the unpieced, dark gray fabric sections.

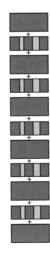

Middle Section

Piece together the paper-pieced blocks, 2 dark gray rectangles 9½″ × 13″, and 4 dark gray rectangles 7″ × 13″ as shown. Press toward the dark gray fabric.

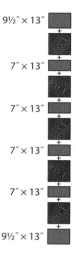

9½″ × 13″
+
+
7″ × 13″
+
+
7″ × 13″
+
+
7″ × 13″
+
+
7″ × 13″
+
+
9½″ × 13″

Section Assembly

Sew together the left section, middle section, and right section as shown in the diagram below. Press the fabric away from the middle section.

Left section   Middle section   Right section

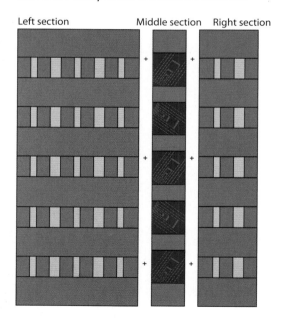

Finishing the Quilt

Baste, quilt, and bind using your favorite methods. Refer to Finishing Your Quilts (page 22) as needed.

SUGGESTED QUILTING OPTIONS

Emily quilted straight-line rectangles inside the light gray fabric pieces, echoing the edges of the rectangles and moving these lines horizontally along the row of rectangles. To break up the angular feel to the quilt and its quilting, she then quilted large-scale bubbles in the dark gray background of the quilt. Stitching in-the-ditch in the paper-pieced blocks, along with some additional decorative straight-line stitching, provided extra reinforcement for the linen fabric. This quilting approach kept the quilt looking masculine—no roses needed for this bachelor.

Looking for something else?

- Quilt organic straight lines at random widths vertically down the quilt. Use a variety of thread colors and thicknesses to add interest.

- If you use a light-colored solid fabric for the background that easily shows quilting patterns, you can showcase your beautiful quilting skills, shifting from one free-motion quilting design to another. This option provides a wonderful amount of texture and additional interest to the simple background of the quilt.

This quilting approach kept the quilt looking masculine—no roses needed for this bachelor.

LITTLE ITTY BITTIES

FINISHED QUILT: 42″ × 42″

Do small scraps of fabric seem to accumulate at your feet? Here's a great pattern to use up even the littlest of your itty-bitty pieces. The largest triangles are 6″ × 3″ and the smallest are a mere ½″ × ⅓″. Paper piecing makes it easy to achieve precision every time, even with such tiny scraps.

Materials

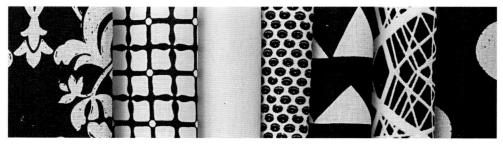

I used a variety of Echino prints mixed in with other cream-and-black prints from my stash. I thought that pairing them with a light pink solid brought a rather retro vibe to the quilt.

Pink: 3⅓ yards (for background)

Black-and-white prints: 6 fat eighths (for triangles); or use scraps, ranging in size from 1¼″ × 1″ to 6¾″ × 3¾″ (See fat eighth cutting directions for exact sizes—instead of 2 of each piece size, cut a total of 12 of each size.)

Backing: 46″ × 46″

Batting: 46″ × 46″

Binding: ½ yard (for 2½″ binding strips)

Fabric labels or your favorite fabric-marking pen

Patterns: Make 4 copies each of *Little Itty Bitties* patterns A, B, and C (pullout pages P2 and P3) on your favorite paper-piecing paper (or see Tip below for using printer sheets).

TIP

These patterns are large in scale. I suggest copying the patterns onto 2 standard 11″ × 17″ printer sheets and pre-perforating the paper with a dull needle. If you prefer to use paper-piecing paper, just tape together all your parts with painter's tape on the back and clear tape on the front (printed side).

Cutting Directions

WOF = width of fabric

All the fabric pieces are numbered 1–24 (to coordinate with the order in which they are used on the pattern piece). Pieces 23 and 24 are used after the paper-piecing patterns are completed. This quilt uses 3 patterns: A, B, and C. Pieces 1–20 are the same for all the pattern pieces. Pieces 21 and 22 are different, so they are labeled with both the pattern letter and the piece number (for example, A21, A22, B21, and so on). As you cut out the fabric pieces, label each piece with the number or letter/number combination indicated. Keep them in piles organized numerically.

PINK (BACKGROUND):

- Cut 2 strips 7¼″ × WOF. Subcut each strip into 2 rectangles 7¼″ × 10¾″ (Piece A22) and 2 rectangles 7¼″ × 7″ (Piece A21).

- Cut 1 strip 6½″ × WOF. Subcut into 4 rectangles 6½″ × 7″ (Piece C21) and 1 rectangle 6½″ × 7½″ (Piece B22).

- Cut 1 strip 7″ × WOF.

  Subcut into 4 rectangles 7″ × 4″ (Piece B21).

  From the remaining fabric, cut a strip 6½″ × WOF. Subcut into 3 rectangles 6½″ × 7½″ (Piece B22).

- Cut 1 strip 8″ × WOF.

  Subcut into 4 rectangles 8″ × 4″ (Piece C22).

  From the remaining fabric, cut a strip 6½″ × WOF. Subcut into 6 rectangles 6½″ × 4″ (Piece 16).

- Cut 1 strip 4″ wide. Subcut into 6 rectangles 4″ × 6½″ (Piece 16).

- Cut 4 strips 4½″ × WOF.

  Subcut 1 strip into 10 rectangles 4½″ × 4″ (Piece 15).

  Subcut 1 strip into 2 rectangles 4½″ × 4″ (Piece 15) and 4 rectangles 4½″ × 7½″ (Piece 19).

  Subcut 2 strips, each into 4 rectangles 4½″ × 7½″ (Piece 19) and 3 rectangles 4½″ × 3″. Cut each 4½″ × 3″ rectangle in half to have a total of 12 rectangles 2¼″ × 3″ (Piece 4).

- Cut 3 strips 4½″ × WOF.

  Subcut 1 strip into 12 rectangles 4½″ × 3″ (Piece 10).

  With the remaining 2 strips, subcut each strip into 6 rectangles 4½″ × 5¾″ (Piece 18) and 2 rectangles 4½″ × 1¾″. Cut each 4½″ × 1¾″ rectangle into thirds to have a total of 12 rectangles 1½″ × 1¾″ (Piece 1).

- Cut 3 strips 3¼″ × WOF. Subcut each strip into 4 rectangles 3¼″ × 5½″ (Piece 13) and 4 rectangles 3¼″ × 3¾″ (Piece 12).

- Cut 2 strips 2½″ × WOF. Subcut each strip into 6 rectangles 2½″ × 3¾″ (Piece 7) and 6 squares 2½″ × 2½″ (Piece 6).

- Cut 1 strip 3″ × WOF. Subcut into 12 squares 3″ × 3″ (Piece 9).

- Cut 1 strip 2″ × WOF. Subcut into 12 rectangles 2″ × 2¼″ (Piece 3).

- From the remaining fabric:

  Cut 2 squares 16⅞". Subcut into HSTs (half-square triangles) by cutting in half diagonally, corner to corner (Piece 24).

  Cut 2 squares 3⅛". Subcut into HSTs by cutting in half diagonally, corner to corner (Piece 23).

BLACK-AND-WHITE FABRICS:

Use the cutting guide (at right) to cut the following pieces from each fat eighth:

- Cut 2 rectangles 6¾" × 3¾" (Piece 20).

- Cut 2 rectangles 5¼" × 3" (Piece 17).

- Cut 2 rectangles 4" × 2½" (Piece 14).

- Cut 2 rectangles 3" × 2" (Piece 11).

- Cut 2 rectangles 2¼" × 1½" (Piece 8).

- Cut 2 rectangles 1¾" × 1¼" (Piece 5).

- Cut 2 rectangles 1¼" × 1" (Piece 2).

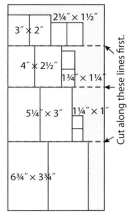

TIP

I could tell that some of the prints would not translate well to the smallest triangle pieces, so I doubled up on other prints for Pieces 2 and 5.

Cutting guide for black-and-white fabrics

Little Itty Bitties, 42" × 42", pieced and quilted by Amy Garro

Quilt Top Construction

PAPER-PIECING ASSEMBLY

Sew each printed paper-piecing pattern. Begin with Piece 1 and work your way through Piece 11 on each pattern. Press the seams open after piecing. Refer to Paper-Piecing Basics (page 12) as needed.

While piecing, I made sure to limit the number of prints repeated within each pattern piece. After stitching the first 9 paper foundations, I laid them out and moved them around until I found a pleasing arrangement. Then I chose the exact placement of the triangles for the remaining 3 pattern pieces before piecing them. This helped me avoid lots of the same fabrics clumping up in one area.

PIECING TOGETHER THE WEDGES

1. Sew together groups of 3 wedge sections, with Wedge A in the middle and Wedges B and C on each side. Sew from the inside to the outside (from the narrow end to the wide end).

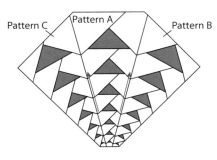

Pattern C   Pattern A   Pattern B

2. Position the inner triangles (Piece 23) by folding the edges of the triangles together and finger-pressing to form a crease in the center of the longest side. Fold the edges of each wedge together and finger-press to form a crease in the center of Wedge A.

Match the center creases, pin, and sew. Press the seams open.

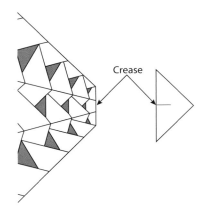

Crease

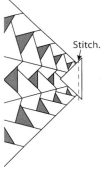

Stitch.

3. Sew together the 4 quarters.

4. Position the outer triangles (Piece 24) by finger-pressing the edges of the triangles and finger-pressing to form a crease in the center of the longest side. Match the center crease of the triangle to the seam between Pieces B and C. Pin and sew. Press the seams open.

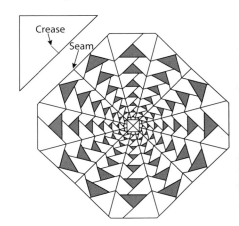

Crease   Seam

Scant ¼" seam should hit where the 2 pieces meet.

Line up crease and seam.

Finishing the Quilt

Baste, quilt, and bind using your favorite methods. Refer to Finishing Your Quilts (page 22) as needed.

SUGGESTED QUILTING OPTIONS

This quilt has two very distinct features—the circular layout and the angular triangles. When choosing your quilt design, you might try to play off of one of these features to emphasize it.

I quilted my version with a circular version of Pebbles in a Stream, a pattern that I found on Leah Day's website (freemotionquilting.blogspot.com). This helps draw the viewers' eyes to the circular layout. I felt it also helped distract the viewer's eye from the "seamy" look of the background of the quilt.

Other ideas to try:

- Hand quilt with a chunky, contrasting perle cotton #8 thread around the triangles and machine quilt a stipple pattern in the background with a thread color that blends in.

- An allover pattern that mimics either the circular layout or the triangles, such as swirls or meandering triangles, would work well also.

This quilt has two very distinct features—the circular layout and the angular triangles.

TIED DOWN

Masculine fabrics are made to resemble men's ties braided down this bed quilt. The pattern calls for 3˝ wide strips, but if you're a practiced paper piecer, you can get away with 2½˝ strips easily, turning this into a great jelly roll project.

Materials

I used a Botanicals textural solid for the background with a variety of Parson Gray fabrics for the braids. The Parson Gray fabrics actually came from multiple fabric lines. While it is common to work from within a single line for a quilt, I find that many designers have fabrics from different lines that work well with each other. By pulling from 2 or 3 lines (as availability allows), you have a wider range of options at your hands, while still keeping the same feel between all the prints.

TIP

Are you a confident piecer? Try making a block with 2½˝ × 8˝ strips. If this size works for you, then you can use jelly rolls for this project. You'll need at least 46 jelly roll–sized strips. Subcut each strip into 5 rectangles 2½˝ × 8˝. Continue with the cutting directions for the background fabric as usual.

Gray: 5⅛ yards (for background)

Prints: 9 or more assorted (ties), ⅝ yard each

TIP

I used 14 prints to have a greater variety of prints and simply had extra fabric. You can certainly change the number of fabrics you use. You will need a minimum total of 227 individual print pieces to complete the project. I suggest having at least 5–10 additional pieces cut to make those last few pieces easy to place without worrying about repeating prints or ending up with a group of prints that don't look pleasing right next to each other. You actually only need 9 prints, so cutting directions for both 9 and 14 prints are included.

Backing: 76″ × 93″

Batting: 76″ × 93″

Binding: ⅔ yard (for 2½″-wide binding strips)

Fabric labels or your favorite fabric-marking pen

Patterns: Make 10 copies of *Tied Down* beginning pattern piece (pullout page P4), 38 copies of *Tied Down* middle pattern piece (pullout page P4), 5 copies of *Tied Down* end Piece A (pullout page P3), and 5 copies of *Tied Down* end Piece B (pullout page P3) on your favorite 8½″ × 11″ paper-piecing paper.

Cutting Directions

WOF = width of fabric; LOF = length of fabric

All the fabric pieces are assigned a number (to coordinate with the order in which they are used on the pattern piece). As you cut out the fabric pieces, label each piece with the number indicated. Keep them in piles organized by their labels

GRAY (BACKGROUND):

Cut 2 sections 85½" × WOF.

NOTE

The strips needed for this project are very long, so after cutting the 2 initial WOF sections, you will cut the strips parallel to the selvage—or the length of the fabric instead of the standard WOF. Here, the LOF will always be 85½".

FROM FIRST SECTION:

- Cut 1 strip 6½" × LOF.

- Cut 1 strip 6" × LOF.

- Cut 1 strip 4" × LOF.

- Cut 1 strip 3½" × LOF.

- Cut 1 strip 3" × LOF.

- Cut 2 strips 5½" × LOF.

- Cut 2 strips 2½" × LOF.

FROM SECOND SECTION:

- Cut 1 strip 2½" × LOF.

- Cut 1 strip 2" × LOF.

- Cut 5 strips 3½" × LOF.

Subcut 1 strip into 1 strip 3½" × 71" (Strip 4) and 1 strip 3½" × 7" (Strip 7).

Subcut 1 strip into 1 strip 3½" × 47" (Strip 9) and 1 strip 3½" × 31" (Strip 1).

Subcut 1 strip into 1 strip 3½" × 45" (Strip 3) and 1 strip 3½" × 31" (Strip 6).

Subcut 2 strips into 1 strip 3½" × 61" (Strips 5 and 10) and 1 strip 3½" × 21" (Strips 2 and 8) each.

FROM REMAINING FABRIC:

- Cut 1 strip 7" × WOF. Subcut into 10 rectangles 3½" × 7" (second-to-last piece).

- Cut 1 strip 5" × WOF. Subcut into 10 rectangles 2½" × 5" (last piece).

TIP

I used a directional fabric for my background, so I opted to create a cutting template to keep the pattern running in the same direction (see Tip: Using Directional Fabrics, page 21).

PRINTS:

OPTION 1—FROM EACH OF 9 ASSORTED PRINTS:

- Cut 2 strips 8" × WOF. Subcut each strip into 13 rectangles 8" × 3". (From all the prints, you will have a total of 234 strips, with 7 extra.)

OPTION 2—FROM EACH OF 14 ASSORTED PRINTS:

- Cut 2 strips 8" × WOF.

Subcut 1 strip into 13 rectangles 8" × 3".

Subcut 1 strip into 4 rectangles 8" × 3".

(From all the prints, you will have a total of 238 strips, with 11 extra.)

Tied Down, 68″ × 85″, pieced by Amy Garro; quilted by Angela Walters

Quilt Top Construction

Each braid is made of multiple pattern pieces. To help you keep everything organized, an area is provided on the top of the first pattern piece of each braid for recording important information. As you sew, make sure your braided sections match up the layout diagram. Because the number of pattern pieces varies with each braid, only the first pattern is numbered. If desired, you can continue numbering the added pattern pieces in the lines provided on the pattern.

PAPER-PIECING ASSEMBLY

NOTE

Connecting/Adding Pattern Pieces: Some of the braids end up being very long—the longest is composed of 10 pattern pieces. You may certainly assemble all the pattern pieces for each braid before you begin paper piecing, but it's easier to assemble them as you go so you don't have extra paper to work with. To help you remember to add the next pattern piece, I've written "Attach next pattern piece before sewing this seam" directly on all the patterns to prompt you. At that point in time, you will simply tape the next pattern piece to the one you are currently working on. Tape lightly on both the front and back of the pattern, avoiding taping down any fabric. Overlap the patterns as indicated by the pattern piece. Then, continue until you are ready to add your End Pattern A or B. With these patterns, you will simply sew to the end—no need to worry about attaching another pattern piece.

Construct each braid by sewing on the number of patterns in the order indicated, adding pattern pieces as you reach the indicated seamline. Begin with Piece 1 and work your way up numerically on each pattern. Press the seams open after everything is pieced. Refer to Paper-Piecing Basics (page 12) as needed.

Braid 1

Patterns needed (7 total):
1 Beginning Pattern Piece,
5 Middle Pattern Pieces,
1 End Pattern Piece A

Braid 2

Patterns needed (8 total):
1 Beginning Pattern Piece,
6 Middle Pattern Pieces,
1 End Pattern Piece B

Braid 3

Patterns needed (5 total):
1 Beginning Pattern Piece,
3 Middle Pattern Pieces,
1 End Pattern Piece B

Braid 4

Patterns needed (2 total):
1 Beginning Pattern Piece,
1 End Pattern Piece A

Braid 5

Patterns needed (3 total):
1 Beginning Pattern Piece,
1 Middle Pattern Piece,
1 End Pattern Piece B

Braid 6

Patterns needed (7 total):
1 Beginning Pattern Piece,
5 Middle Pattern Pieces,
1 End Pattern Piece A

Braid 7

Patterns needed (10 total): 1 Beginning Pattern Piece, 8 Middle Pattern Pieces, 1 End Pattern Piece A

Braid 8

Patterns needed (8 total): 1 Beginning Pattern Piece, 6 Middle Pattern Pieces, 1 End Pattern Piece B

Braid 9

Patterns needed (5 total): 1 Beginning Pattern Piece, 3 Middle Pattern Pieces, 1 End Pattern Piece A

Braid 10

Patterns needed (3 total): 1 Beginning Pattern Piece, 1 Middle Pattern Piece, 1 End Pattern Piece B

LAYOUT AND FINAL ASSEMBLY

1. After paper piecing each braid, sew Strips 1–10 to the correlating braid: sew Strip 1 to Braid 1, Strip 2 to Braid 2, and so on. Sew together along the 3½″ side. Press the seams away from the braided pieces.

2. Assemble the quilt top by stitching the strips with the braids to the plain 85½″ strips. Use the quilt assembly diagram (below), which indicates the width of the 85½″ strips, to aid in assembly. Press the seams away from the braided pieces (toward 85½″ strips).

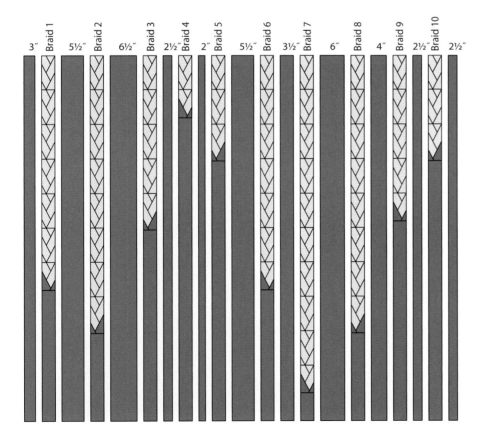

TIP

Sewing together a large number of long strips can cause drifting and curving. To combat both of these problems, sew each seam in the opposite direction. Good pinning will also prevent excessive shifting. If you find that shifting has occurred, you can always square up your quilt.

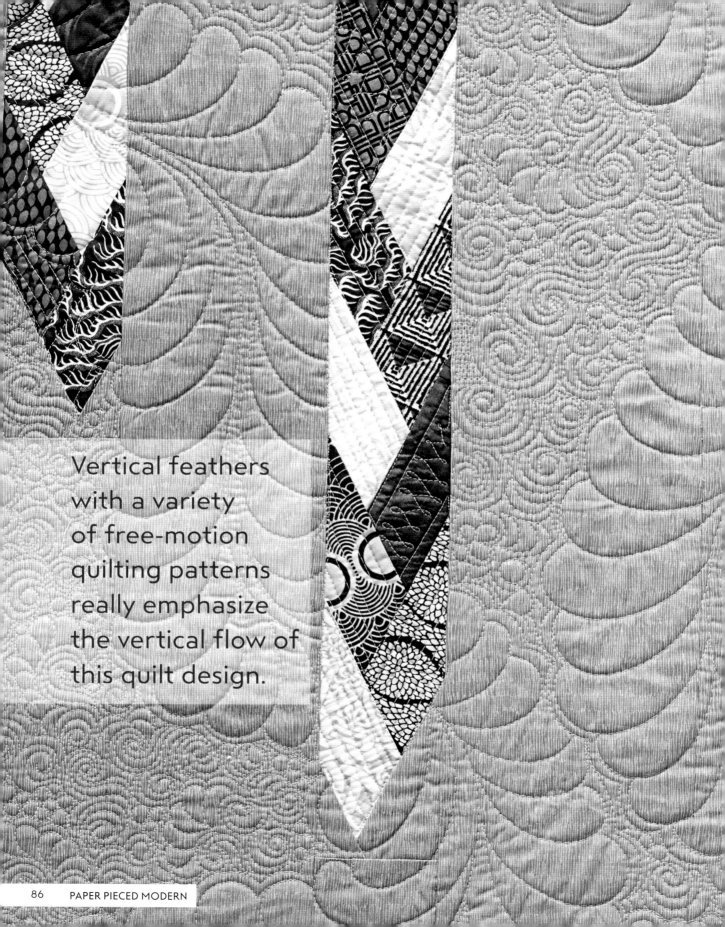

Vertical feathers
with a variety
of free-motion
quilting patterns
really emphasize
the vertical flow of
this quilt design.

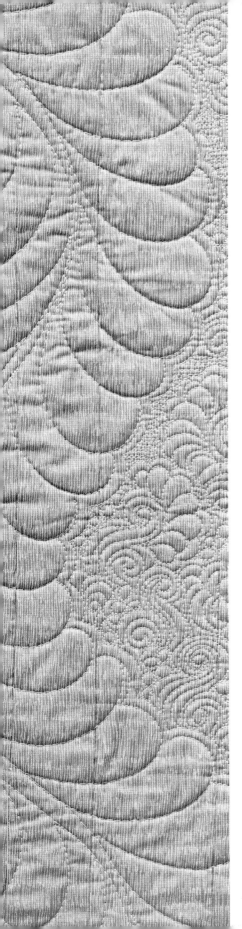

Finishing the Quilt

Baste, quilt, and bind using your favorite methods. Refer to Finishing Your Quilts (page 22) as needed.

SUGGESTED QUILTING OPTIONS

- I asked Angela to quilt some vertical feathers with a variety of free-motion quilting patterns between the feathers. This really emphasizes the vertical flow of this quilt design, while giving a great texture to all that negative space.

- If you're going for a snowy feel with icicle-colored braids, try swirls and pebbles—they'll look like wind and snow.

- If you're looking for a quicker quilting option, vertical straight-line quilting would work well with this project. Use a serpentine or wavy stitch to give the design some extra interest.

FACETED JEWELS I

FINISHED QUILT: 65″ × 84″

Modern traditionalism, anyone? This quilt breaks into the modern quilting realm with plenty of negative space and asymmetry, but also has traditional roots. You need only four prints for this project; the jewels sparkle from the placement of the different values.

Materials

I used Kona White, Parson Gray Curious Nature, and Tula Pink Salt Water prints for this version of Faceted Jewels. Including the white background, you will need 4 values. I chose white, a black print, and 2 blues for the middle-value prints. The center squares of the jewels can be made with a fabric of any value; I opted for another middle-value print.

White: 5½ yards (for background)

Black: ⅞ yard

Dark blue: 1¾ yards

Light blue: 1⅜ yards

Medium blue: ¼ yard (for center squares)

Backing: 73″ × 92″

Batting: 73″ × 92″

Binding: ¾ yard (for 2½″-wide binding strips)

Fabric labels or your favorite fabric-marking pen

Patterns: Make 40 copies of the *Faceted Jewels I* pattern (pullout page P2) on your favorite 11″ × 17″ or 8½″ × 11″ paper-piecing paper. Tape together with painter's or masking tape and trim as necessary.

Cutting Directions

WOF = width of fabric; LOF = length of fabric

All the fabric pieces are assigned a number (to coordinate with the order in which they are used on the pattern piece). As you cut out the fabric pieces, label each piece with the number indicated. Keep them in piles organized by their labels.

WHITE (BACKGROUND):

- Cut a section 90″ × WOF from the white yardage.

- Cut 1 strip 3½″ × LOF. Trim to 84½″ long (Section 26).

- From the remaining fabric in this cut of yardage:

  Cut 1 strip 12⅞″ × WOF. Subcut into 2 squares 12⅞″ × 12⅞″. Subcut each square in half diagonally, corner to corner, to make 4 HSTs (half-square triangles). Set aside.

  Cut 1 strip 24½″ × WOF. Subcut into 1 rectangle 24½″ × 26½″ (Section 7) and 1 rectangle 24½″ × 2½″ (Section 17).

  Cut 1 strip 26½″ × WOF. Subcut into 1 rectangle 26½″ × 36½″ (Section 25).

  Cut 1 strip 12½″ × WOF. Subcut into 1 rectangle 12½″ × 36½″ (Section 24).

  Cut 1 strip 12½″ × WOF. Subcut into 1 rectangle 12½″ × 24½″ (Section 12).

- Return to the remaining white fabric.

  Cut 2 strips 12⅞″ × WOF. Subcut each strip into 3 squares 12⅞″ × 12⅞″; then subcut each square in half diagonally, corner to corner, to make 12 HSTs. Set aside with the other HSTs.

  Cut 2 strips 8½″ × WOF. Subcut each strip into 17 rectangles 8½″ × 2¼″ (Piece 4).

  Cut 1 strip 9″ × WOF. Subcut into 6 rectangles 9″ × 2¼″ (Piece 5). Trim remaining section to 8½″ wide; then subcut into 6 rectangles 8½″ × 2¼″ (Piece 4).

  Cut 2 strips 9″ × WOF. Subcut each strip into 17 rectangles 9″ × 2¼″ (Piece 5).

  Cut 16 strips 2″ × WOF. Subcut each strip into 5 rectangles 2″ × 8″ (Pieces 7 and 8).

  Cut 1 strip 12½″ × WOF. Subcut into 2 squares 12½″ × 12½″ (Sections 1 and 21) and 6 rectangles 12″ × 2½″ (Piece 1).

BLACK:

- Cut 5 strips 2½″ × WOF.

  Subcut 4 strips, each into 3 rectangles 2½″ × 12″ (Piece 6).

  Subcut 1 strip into 2 rectangles 2½″ × 12″ (Piece 1) and 2 rectangles 2″ × 7½″ (Piece 2).

- Cut 2 strips 2″ × WOF. Subcut each strip into 5 rectangles 2″ × 7½″ (Piece 2).

- Cut 3 strips 3″ × WOF. Subcut each strip into 4 rectangles 3″ × 10″ (Piece 3).

DARK BLUE:

- Cut 11 strips 2½″ × WOF.

  Subcut 10 strips, each into 3 rectangles 2½″ × 12″ (16 Piece 1; the remaining are Piece 6).

  Subcut 1 strip into 2 rectangles 2½″ × 12″ (Piece 6) and 1 rectangle 2″ × 7½″ (Piece 2).

- Cut 3 strips 2″ × WOF. Subcut each strip into 5 rectangles 2″ × 7½″ (Piece 2).

- Cut 4 strips 3″ × WOF. Subcut each strip into 4 rectangles 3″ × 10″ (Piece 3).

LIGHT BLUE:

- Cut 10 strips 2½″ × WOF.

  Subcut 9 strips, each into 3 rectangles 2½″ × 12″ (16 Pieces 1; the remaining are Pieces 6).

  Subcut 1 strip into 1 rectangle 2½″ × 12″ (Piece 6) and 2 rectangles 2″ × 7½″ (Piece 2).

- Cut 2 strips 2″ × WOF. Subcut each strip into 5 rectangles 2″ × 7½″ (Piece 2).

- Cut 3 strips 3″ × WOF. Subcut each strip into 4 rectangles 3″ × 10″ (Piece 3).

MEDIUM BLUE (CENTER SQUARES):

- Cut 2 strips 2½″ × WOF. Subcut each strip into 20 squares 2½″ × 2½″ (Piece 9).

TIP

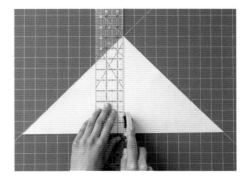

If your ruler isn't long enough to reach diagonally across the 12⅞″ HSTs, you can fold the squares diagonally to cut them. Line up your square with the 45° lines on your cutting mat. Fold it in half. Place the ruler straight up and down, matching it to the corner of the square and the vertical line on your cutting mat that hits the corner. Cut as usual.

Faceted Jewels I, 65″ × 84″, pieced by Amy Garro; quilted by Emily Sessions

Quilt Top Construction

PAPER-PIECING ASSEMBLY

Sew each printed paper-piecing pattern, referring to the diagram below as necessary. Begin with Piece 1 and work your way through Piece 8 on each pattern. Press the seams open after piecing. Refer to Paper-Piecing Basics (page 12) as needed.

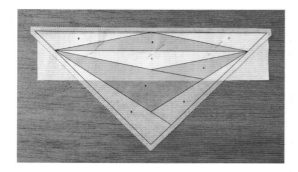

Tricky Pieces

Pieces 7 and 8 have *jutting corners*. Follow the directions in Jutting Corners (page 17) to place your fabric correctly.

Quadrant A: Make 10.

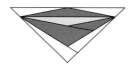

Quadrant D: Make 14.

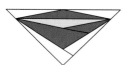

Quadrant B: Make 2.

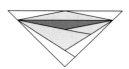

Quadrant E: Make 6.

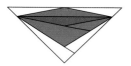

Quadrant C: Make 2.

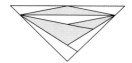

Quadrant F: Make 6.

BLOCK ASSEMBLY

1. Make 10 Quadrants A using dark blue for Piece 1; black for Pieces 2, 3, and 6; and white for Pieces 4, 5, 7, and 8.

2. Make 2 Quadrants B using light blue for Piece 1; black for Pieces 2, 3, and 6; and white for Pieces 4, 5, 7, and 8.

3. Make 2 Quadrants C using black for Piece 1; dark blue for Pieces 2, 3, and 6; and white for Pieces 4, 5, 7, and 8.

4. Make 14 Quadrants D using light blue for Piece 1; dark blue for Pieces 2, 3, and 6; and white for Pieces 4, 5, 7, and 8.

5. Make 6 Quadrants E using dark blue for Piece 1; light blue for Pieces 2, 3, and 6; and white for Pieces 4, 5, 7, and 8.

6. Make 6 Quadrants F using white for Piece 1; light blue for Pieces 2, 3, and 6; and white for Pieces 4, 5, 7, and 8.

ASSEMBLING THE SECTIONS

This quilt is assembled into 26 sections; then the sections are sewn together. Use the basic instructions and the diagrams (below) to assemble each section.

Section 2

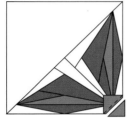

1. Sew together 2 Quadrants A. Press the seams open.

2. Sew a white HST to the quadrants. Press the seams open.

3. On the wrong side of a Piece 9 (medium blue square), draw a line diagonally, corner to corner. Place the piece on the assembled section as shown in the diagram (above), right sides together. Sew along the marked line. Trim ¼″ away from the seam. Press the fabric toward the corner triangle.

Sections 3, 4, 6, 8, 9, 10, 11, 13, 14, 15, 16, 18, 20, 22, 23

Use the layout and assembly diagram (page 94) to assemble these sections in the same manner as Section 2.

Section 5

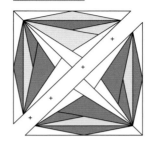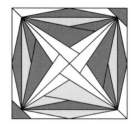

1. Sew together 2 Quadrants D. Press the seams open.

2. Sew together a Quadrant D and a Quadrant E. Press the seams open.

3. Sew the 2 sections together as shown in the diagram (above).

4. Sew 2 Pieces 9 onto the assembled section as shown in the Section 2 diagram (at left), following the directions in Section 2, Step 3.

Section 19

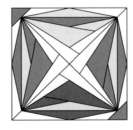

Use the diagram (above) to assemble this section in the same manner as Section 5.

LAYOUT AND FINAL ASSEMBLY

Sew the sections as directed; then sew the 3 completed sections together. After the sections are sewn together, attach Section 26. Press all seams open and refer to the diagram as necessary.

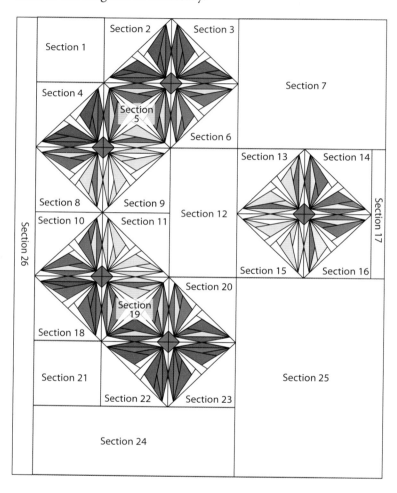

Top Portion

1. Sew together Sections 1, 2, and 3.

2. Sew together Sections 4, 5, and 6.

3. Sew Section 1-2-3 to Section 4-5-6.

4. Sew to Section 7.

Left Middle Portion

1. Sew together Sections 8 and 9.

2. Sew together Sections 10 and 11.

3. Sew Section 8-9 to Section 10-11.

4. Sew to Section 12.

Right Middle Portion

1. Sew together Sections 13 and 14.

2. Sew together Sections 15 and 16.

3. Sew Section 13-14 to Section 15-16.

4. Sew to Section 17.

Bottom Portion

1. Sew together Sections 18, 19, and 20.

2. Sew together Sections 21, 22, and 23.

3. Sew Section 18-19-20 to Section 21-22-23.

4. Sew to Section 24.

5. Sew to Section 25.

Finishing the Quilt

Baste, quilt, and bind using your favorite methods. Refer to Finishing Your Quilts (page 22) as needed.

SUGGESTED QUILTING OPTIONS

- Emily used straight lines at a variety of angles to create some unique, yet subtle, patterns in the background of this quilt; she stitched in-the-ditch of the blocks themselves for stability. This complemented the pattern of the quilt without overwhelming it.

- Quilt "ghost blocks" (outlines of the blocks that you actually pieced) in the negative space and fill in the surrounding areas with a variety of free-motion quilting fillers to make the ghost blocks pop.

- Quilt straight, converging lines radiating out from a single point on the quilt. Choose an off-center starting point to mirror the off-center composition of the quilt.

- Quilt large-scale feathers wrapping throughout the negative space around the blocks. Fill in around the feathers with dense straight-line quilting.

Stitch in-the-ditch gives the blocks stability without overwhleming the pattern of the quilt.

JUMPING JACKS

FINISHED BLOCK: 8″ × 12″
FINISHED QUILT: 48″ × 64″

This fun, nautical quilt brightens up any kid's room. The negative space provides a resting place for your eye to balance out the busy pattern. Coordinating quilts, with similar fabric and color choices, are a great way to bring together a shared children's bedroom without matching everything exactly.

Materials

I used Michael Miller solids in Paprika and Brick, Dear Stella Tiny Diamonds in Navy, Sarah Jane Out to Sea Anchors in Gray, and Michael Miller Tiny Tea Dot Red on White for this quilt. I also made an alternate colorway (page 101) where I used blue fabric for the jacks and white for the background. Experiment with adding your own favorite colors.

White polka dot print: 1¼ yards (for background)

Gray print: ⅝ yard

Light red solid: ½ yard

Dark red solid: ½ yard

Navy print: 2⅞ yards

Backing: 56″ × 72″

Batting: 56″ × 72″

Binding: ⅝ yard (for 2½″-wide binding strips)

Fabric labels or your favorite fabric-marking pen

Patterns: Make 4 copies of each *Jumping Jacks* pattern piece (pullout pages P1 and P3) on your favorite 8½″ × 11″ paper-piecing paper. This quilt uses 4 patterns: A, B, C, and D. Pattern Pieces C and D consist of 2 pieces each; tape them together with painter's or masking tape along the dashed lines to complete them.

Cutting Directions

WOF = width of fabric

All the fabric pieces are assigned a letter (A, B, C, or D, to coordinate with the pattern piece) and a number (1 through 9, to coordinate with the order in which they are used on the pattern piece). As you cut out the fabric pieces, label each piece with the letter/number combination indicated. Keep them in piles organized by their labels.

GRAY (BACKGROUND):

- Cut 2 strips 7″ × WOF.

  Subcut each strip into 6 rectangles 6″ × 7″ (4 each Pieces A1, B1, and D1).

  From the remaining fabric, cut 4 squares 3″ × 3″ (Piece C1).

WHITE POLKA DOT:

- Cut 2 strips 2″ × WOF. Subcut each strip into 4 rectangles 2″ × 7½″ (4 each Pieces A2 and B2).

- Cut 3 strips 2¾″ × WOF. Subcut each strip into 5 rectangles 2¾″ × 8″ (4 each Pieces A3, B3, and D2; 3 Piece D3).

- Cut 1 strip 2″ × WOF. Subcut into 8 rectangles 2″ × 3½″ (4 each Pieces C2 and C3).

- Cut 2 strips 3″ × WOF. Subcut each strip into 4 rectangles 3″ × 7½″. Use the cutting diagram (above right) to cut the corner off of each rectangle (4 each Pieces C8 and C9). Mark the 3¼″ measurement on the width of the fabric pieces. Cut from this mark to the corner. Make 4 of each orientation.

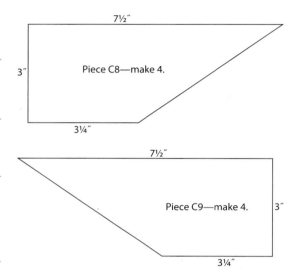

- Cut 2 strips 7″ × WOF. Subcut each strip into 4 rectangles 7″ × 8″. Use the cutting diagram (below) to subcut each rectangle into 2 stubbed triangles (4 each Pieces A9, B9, D8, and D9). Mark the 1½″ measurement on the width of each side of the fabric pieces. Cut from mark to mark as shown below. If using a print, place the fabric right side up and cut half of the rectangles in one orientation and half in the opposite orientation.

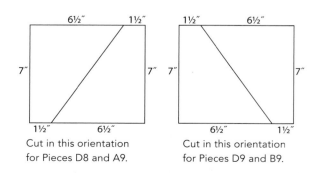

Cut in this orientation for Pieces D8 and A9.

Cut in this orientation for Pieces D9 and B9.

- Cut 1 strip 2½" × WOF.

  Subcut into 8 rectangles 2½" × 3½" (4 each of Pieces A8 and B8).

- From the remaining fabric, cut 1 rectangle 2¾" × 8" (Piece D3).

LIGHT RED SOLID:

- Cut 2 strips 2½" × WOF. Subcut each strip into 4 rectangles 2½" × 9½" (4 each Pieces A5 and D4).

- Cut 2 strips 2¼" × WOF. Subcut each strip into 4 rectangles 2¼" × 10" (4 each Pieces B7 and D7).

- Cut 1 strip 2" × WOF.

  Subcut into 4 rectangles 2" × 5" (Piece C6).

  Trim the remaining amount of the strip to 1¾" wide; then subcut trimmed strip into 4 rectangles 1¾" × 3¾" (Piece C5).

- Cut 1 strip 1½" × WOF.

  Subcut into 4 rectangles 1½" × 5" (Piece B4).

- Trim the remaining amount of the strip to 1¼" wide; then subcut trimmed strip into 4 rectangles 1¼" × 4" (Piece A6).

DARK RED SOLID:

- Cut 1 strip 2" × WOF.

  Subcut into 4 rectangles 2" × 5" (Piece C7).

  Trim the remaining amount of strip to 1½" wide; then subcut trimmed strip into 4 rectangles 1½" × 5" (Piece A4).

- Cut 2 strips 2¼" × WOF. Subcut each strip into 4 rectangles 2¼" × 10" (4 each Pieces A7 and D6).

- Cut 2 strips 2½" × WOF. Subcut each strip into 4 rectangles 2½" × 9½" (4 each Pieces B5 and D5).

- Cut 1 strip 1¾" × WOF.

  Subcut into 4 rectangles 1¾" × 3¾" (Piece C4).

  Trim the remaining amount of strip to 1¼" wide. Subcut the trimmed strip into 4 rectangles 1¼" × 4" (Piece B6).

NAVY PRINT:

- Cut a 48½" length of fabric. Trim to 1 rectangle 48½" × 12½" (Piece E).

- Cut another 48½" length of fabric. Trim to 1 rectangle 48½" × 36½" (Piece F).

Jumping Jacks, 48" × 64", pieced by Helen Kleczynski; quilted by Amy Garro

Quilt Top Construction

PAPER-PIECING ASSEMBLY

Sew each printed paper-piecing pattern. Begin with Piece 1 and work your way through Piece 9 on each pattern. Press each piece open after it is pieced. Refer to Paper-Piecing Basics (page 12) as needed.

Tricky Pieces

Lots of sections on the paper-pieced patterns have *jutting corners.* Follow the directions in Jutting Corners (page 17) to place your fabric correctly.

Placing Pieces C8 and C9

1. Place C8 over its intended location, right side up. Gently line it up with the raw edge of the previous piece (in this case, C6), making sure it will adequately cover the seam allowance area of its intended location.

2. Carefully flip C8 over the edge of the previous fabric piece, being careful not to shift it up or down along the matched edges.

3. Sew and flip open. Press.

4. Repeat Steps 1–3 for Piece C9.

Placing Pieces D8 and D9

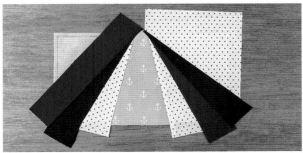

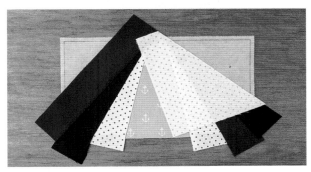

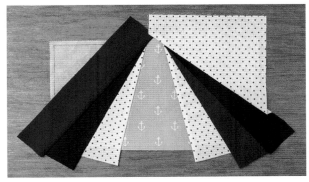

Following the same method as Pieces C8 and C9 (previous page), place, flip, and sew Pieces D8 and D9. Piece D8 is pictured in the photos above.

Jumping Jacks (alternate colorway), 48″ × 64″, pieced by Helen Kleczynski; quilted by Amy Garro

BLOCK ASSEMBLY

1. Sew together Pieces A and B to create 4 Blocks I. Press the seams open to reduce bulk where multiple seams meet.

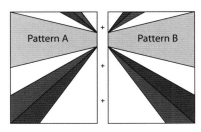

Block I

2. Sew together Pieces C and D to create 4 Blocks II. Press the seams open to reduce bulk where multiple seams meet.

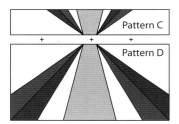

Block II

LAYOUT AND FINAL ASSEMBLY

1. Piece together the Blocks I and II into 2 rows as shown in the diagram. Then, sew together the 2 rows. Press all seams open.

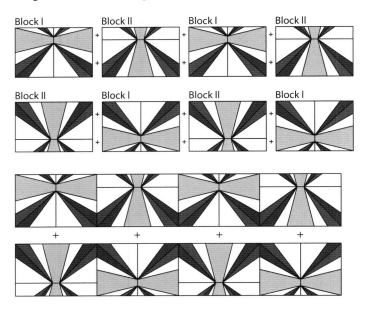

2. Sew Pieces E and F to the top and bottom of the paper-pieced section of the quilt. Press the seams open.

Finishing the Quilt

Baste, quilt, and bind using your favorite methods. Refer to Finishing Your Quilts (page 22) as needed.

SUGGESTED QUILTING OPTIONS

- I quilted random crossing lines horizontally across the quilt with a lightly contrasting thread to add visual interest. My main hope with this pattern was to achieve a nice texture for tiny hands to enjoy. With the main quilt I used 40-weight Sulky rayon thread, and with the alternate colorway (page 101) I opted for 30-weight Sulky cotton thread. The feel and look of each is very different—don't be afraid to try out different thread types.

- Use a contrasting thread to "draw" large waves cascading across the quilt. Then fill in the crests with bubbles.

- Quilt with simple straight lines or a diamond crosshatch to add a lovely texture to the quilt, while keeping it simple for a kid's room.

- Go over the top and quilt seashells, pirate ships, and anchors in the negative space, filling the areas in between with a variety of free-motion fillers.

- Quilt "ghost blocks" (outlines of the blocks that you actually pieced) in the negative space and fill in the surrounding areas with a variety of free-motion quilting fillers to make the ghost blocks pop.

My main hope with this pattern was to achieve a nice texture for tiny hands to enjoy.

FACETED JEWELS II

This quilt uses a variation of the same block found in *Faceted Jewels I* (page 88). It's perfect for a little girl's room when you want to have the striking lines of modern design mixed with the comfort of a traditional quilt. Can't you imagine all the great tea parties that will take place on top of it?

FINISHED BLOCK: 12″ × 12″
FINISHED QUILT: 48″ × 60″

Materials

I used 3 values of 2 different hues (violets and red violets) to create this quilt. The values don't need to correlate exactly between the 2 colors (for example, my lightest red violet is much lighter than my lightest violet) as long as you have one light, medium, and dark value for each.

White: 4½ yards (for background)

Colorway A (red violets):

Light value: Kona Petunia, 1⅛ yards

Medium value: Kona Violet, 1¾ yards

Dark value: Kona Magenta, 1 yard

Colorway B (violets):

Light value: Kona Wisteria, 1⅛ yards

Medium value: Kona Crocus, 1¾ yards

Dark value: Kona Tulip, 1 yard

Backing: 56″ × 68″

Batting: 56″ × 68″

Binding: ½ yard (for 2½″-wide binding strips)

Fabric labels or your favorite fabric-marking pen

Patterns: Make 40 copies of *Faceted Jewels II* patterns A and B (pullout page P4) on your favorite 8½″ × 11″ paper-piecing paper. Cut out both parts of the pattern and tape them together using painter's or masking tape.

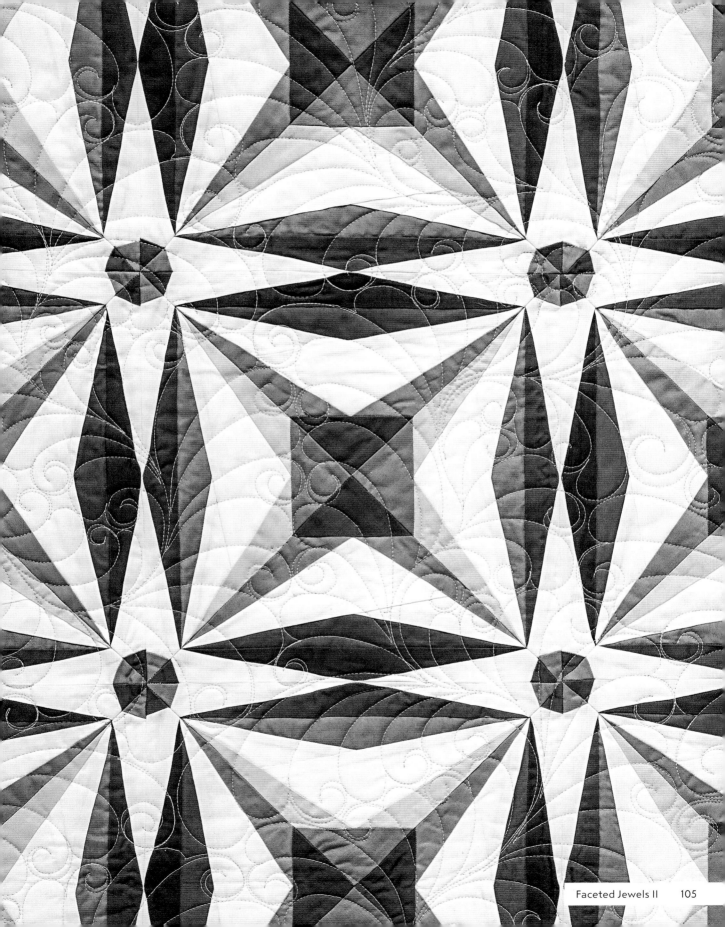

Cutting Directions

WOF = width of fabric

All the fabric pieces are assigned a number (to coordinate with the order in which they are used on the pattern piece). As you cut out the fabric pieces, label each piece with the number indicated. Keep them in piles organized by their labels. Each block is composed of 2 quadrants made in colorway A and 2 quadrants made in colorway B.

WHITE (BACKGROUND):

- Cut 12 strips 7½″ × WOF. Subcut each strip into 20 rectangles 7½″ × 2″ (Pieces A2, B2, A8, A9, B8, and B9).

- Cut 20 strips 3″ × WOF. Subcut each strip into 4 rectangles 3″ × 10″ (Pieces A3 and B3).

COLORWAY A

LIGHT VALUE (PETUNIA):

- Cut 4 strips 8½″ × WOF. Subcut each strip into 20 rectangles 8½″ × 2″ (Pieces A4 and A5).

MEDIUM VALUE (VIOLET):

- Cut 2 strips 12″ × WOF. Subcut each strip into 16 rectangles 12″ × 2½″ (Piece A1).

- Cut 3 strips 2½″ × WOF. Subcut each strip into 3 rectangles 2½″ × 12½″ (Piece A1; this will yield 1 extra piece).

- Cut 5 strips 2½″ × WOF. Subcut each strip into 16 squares 2½″ × 2½″ (Pieces A10 and A11).

- Cut 2 strips 4″ × WOF. Subcut each strip into 10 squares 4″ × 4″. Subcut into HSTs (half-square triangles) by cutting the squares in half diagonally, corner to corner (Piece A6).

DARK VALUE (MAGENTA):

- Cut 2 strips 12″ × WOF. Subcut each strip into 16 rectangles 12″ × 2½″ (Piece A7).

- Cut 3 strips 2½″ × WOF. Subcut each strip into 3 rectangles 2½″ × 12½″ (Piece A7; this will yield 1 extra piece).

LIGHT VALUE (WISTERIA):

- Cut 4 strips 8½″ × WOF. Subcut each strip into 20 rectangles 8½″ × 2″ (Pieces B4 and B5).

MEDIUM VALUE (CROCUS):

- Cut 2 strips 12″ × WOF. Subcut each strip into 16 rectangles 12″ × 2½″ (Piece B1).

- Cut 3 strips 2½″ × WOF. Subcut each strip into 3 rectangles 2½″ × 12½″ (Piece B1; this will yield 1 extra piece).

- Cut 5 strips 2½″ × WOF. Subcut each strip into 16 squares 2½″ × 2½″ (Pieces B10 and B11).

- Cut 2 strips 4″ × WOF. Subcut each strip into 10 squares 4″ × 4″; then subcut each square into HSTs by cutting the squares in half diagonally, corner to corner (Piece B6).

DARK VALUE (TULIP):

- Cut 2 strips 12″ × WOF. Subcut each strip into 16 rectangles 12″ × 2½″ (Piece B7).

- Cut 3 strips 2½″ × WOF. Subcut each strip into 3 rectangles 2½″ × 12½″ (Piece B7; this will yield 1 extra piece).

Faceted Jewels II, 48″ × 60″, pieced by Amy Garro; quilted by Emily Sessions

Quilt Top Construction

PAPER-PIECING ASSEMBLY

Sew each printed paper-piecing pattern. Begin with Piece 1 and work your way through Piece 11 on each pattern. Press each seam open after piecing. Refer to Paper-Piecing Basics (page 12) as needed.

Tricky Pieces

- Many of the pieces in these blocks are triangles with extreme angles. Refer to Extreme Angles (page 17) for more information.

- Piece 1 is very long and skinny, so pin it carefully. You don't want the pins to cross over into the locations for Pieces 2 and 3, so angle them accordingly.

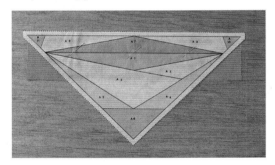

- Piece 10 and Piece 11 have *jutting corners*. Follow the directions in Jutting Corners (page 17) to place your fabric correctly.

BLOCK ASSEMBLY

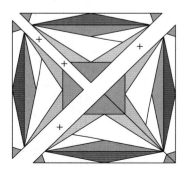

1. Piece together 1 Pattern A and 1 Pattern B to create a half-block. Press the seams open, using a firm hand where multiple seams meet. If needed, press the seams open a second time from the front of the block after pressing them open from the back.

2. Piece together 2 half-blocks to create an entire block. Press the seams open in the same manner as in Step 1. Make sure every block has the same value placement as shown in the block assembly diagram (below left).

LAYOUT AND FINAL ASSEMBLY

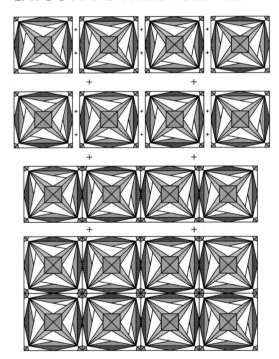

1. Piece 20 blocks total. Arrange the blocks into 5 rows of 4 blocks. Rotate every other block, as shown in the layout and assembly diagram (above), to alternate color placement.

2. When pleased with your arrangement, sew the blocks into rows. Then sew the rows together.

Finishing the Quilt

Baste, quilt, and bind using your favorite methods. Refer to Finishing Your Quilts (page 22) as needed.

SUGGESTED QUILTING OPTIONS

This quilt is seam heavy. Try choosing quilting options that allow you to avoid the bulkiest areas; this will make your life a little easier.

- An allover curvy pattern is a great option to soften this angular quilt. Emily quilted a meandering feathery pattern to bring just the right girly, floral touches to this purple quilt.

- Diagonal straight-line quilting quietly echoes the lines found in the blocks without detracting from the intense pattern.

ABOUT THE AUTHOR

Photo by Amanda Fales-Shaw

AMY GARRO is a modern quilter who lives in Indianapolis with her husband and three children. Her quilting journey began in elementary school, when she learned how to sew from her artist mother. After sewing garments for years, Amy began her first bed-sized quilt in high school, but it took six years to finish it and give it to her now husband as a gift. She eventually started making baby quilts as gifts for friends. After she learned how to machine quilt, she picked up speed, left garment sewing behind, and dove right in to quilting.

Amy took art classes in college and now draws heavily on her design experiences while planning quilts. With her type A personality, Amy especially loves the precision that paper piecing offers and loves to make masculine quilts, often inspired by her husband's engineering designs and sketches. Amy spends her days taking care of her three little boys and her nights (and the boys' nap times) working on quilts. When she's not changing diapers or singing silly songs, you can find her at her local quilt shops, the Indianapolis Modern Quilt Guild, or her sewing machine.

Read more from Amy on her blog, *13 Spools* (13spools.com).

QUILTING RESOURCES

There are many, many online quilting resources. Three of my favorite sites contain a lot of beautiful images for inspiration:

- *The Free Motion Quilting Project* blog by Leah Day (freemotionquilting.blogspot.com)

- *Green Fairy Quilts* blog by Judi Madsen (www.greenfairyquiltsblog.com)

- *Quilting Is My Therapy* blog by Angela Walters (quiltingismytherapy.com)

Below are a few resources from Stash Books:

- *Beginner's Guide to Free-Motion Quilting* by Natalia Bonner

- *First Steps to Free-Motion Quilting* by Christina Cameli

- *Free-Motion Quilting with Angela Walters* by Angela Walters

- *In the Studio with Angela Walters* by Angela Walters

stashBOOKS®

fabric arts for a handmade lifestyle

If you're craving beautiful authenticity in a time of mass-production...Stash Books is for you. Stash Books is a line of how-to books celebrating fabric arts for a handmade lifestyle. Backed by C&T Publishing's solid reputation for quality, Stash Books will inspire you with contemporary designs, clear and simple instructions, and engaging photography.

ctpub.com